The Fortifications of Nafplio

The Fortifications of Nafplio

Allan Brooks

Aetos Press

Copyright © Allan Brooks 2019

First published 2019 by Aetos Press
36 Moor Lane, Huddersfield, HD8 0QS, UK

All rights reserved. No part of this publication may be reproduced, stored in a retrieval system or transmitted in any form or by any means, electronic, mechanical, photocopying, recording or otherwise, without the prior permission, in writing, of the publisher.

ISBN 978-0-9575846-2-4

British Library Cataloguing-in-Publication Data
A catalogue record for this book is available from the British Library.

Aetos Press has no responsibility for the persistence or accuracy of URLs for third-party internet websites referenced in this book, and does not guarantee that any content on these websites is, or will remain, accurate or appropriate.

www.aetospress.co.uk

Contents

List of Figures vi
List of Maps and Plans ix
Preface xi

Introduction 1

1 **The lower town**
   The development of the fortifications 11
   The town walls today 22

2 **The Castle of the Rock (The Bourtzi)** 33

3 **The Acropolis**
   The development of the fortifications 41
   The fortifications of the acropolis today 49

4 **The Palamidi forts** 66
   The Maschio (Fort Robert) 69
   Bastione S. Girardo (Fort Andreas) 75
   Mezzo-baloardo S. Agostino (Fort Themistokles) 82
   The Doppia Tenaglia (Fort Achilles) 91
   The Turkish bastion (Fort Phokion) 97
   Bastione Staccato (Fort Miltiades) 102
   The Piattaforma (Fort Leonidas) 107
   Fort Epaminondas 112

5 **Drepanon Fort** 118

6 **Castle of Thermisi** 123

7 **Summary** 132

Bibliography 136

Index 138

Figures

1.1	Polygonal walling in the lower town.	13
1.2	Grimani bastion.	19
1.3	Southern caponier beneath the rocks of Palamidi.	19
1.4	Surviving section of the sea walls to the south of the Five Brothers bastion.	23
1.5	Walled-up gate of the Grotto.	23
1.6	Interior of the gate of the Ovens.	24
1.7	A section of the foundations of the demolished sea wall.	25
1.8	The restored Land gate.	26
1.9	Grimani bastion: North face.	27
1.10	Grimani bastion: Interior below Castel del Toro.	28
2.1	Castle of the Rock (the Bourtzi) from the south.	35
2.2	The Bourtzi: East battery and barbican.	35
2.3	The Bourtzi: Interior of the barbican.	36
2.4	The Bourtzi: Sea gate.	37
2.5	The Bourtzi: North gate tower.	38
2.6	The Bourtzi: The central tower.	38
3.1	Acronauplia: Walls at the northwest of the circuit.	42
3.2	Acronauplia: Inner face of the east gate.	42
3.3	Acronauplia: Gambello traverse and entrance complex.	45
3.4	Acronauplia: Sally port in the flank of Castel del Toro.	46
3.5	Acronauplia: Dolfin demi-bastion.	48
3.6	Acronauplia: Sagredo gate.	48
3.7	Acronauplia c. 1930.	50
3.8	Acropolis fortifications in 2014.	50
3.9	Acronauplia: Gun batteries of Castel del Toro.	51
3.10	Acronauplia: Pasqualigo's gate to Castel del Toro.	52
3.11	Castle of the Franks: East wall and Venetian talus.	53
3.12	Castle of the Franks: The Venetian gate of 1471.	55
3.13	Gambello traverse: Outer gate of the entrance complex.	56
3.14	Gambello traverse: Inner court of the entrance.	57
3.15	Castle of the Franks: Base of the Frankish tower.	58

Figures

3.16	Acronauplia: Interior stairway of the Sagredo gate.	59
3.17	Acronauplia: The western gun battery.	60
3.18	Acronauplia: Morosini's western gate.	61
3.19	Acronauplia: World War II gun emplacement.	62
3.20	Acronauplia: World War II observation post.	62
4.1	Maschio tower: Lower gate.	71
4.2	Maschio tower: Exterior face.	71
4.3	Screen wall connecting the Maschio to S. Girardo.	72
4.4	Maschio tower: Gun ports.	73
4.5	Powder magazine above the Maschio tower.	74
4.6	Upper gate at the head of the Palamidi stairs.	74
4.7	S. Girardo bastion: The northwest face.	77
4.8	S. Girardo bastion: West demi-bastion.	77
4.9	S. Girardo bastion: Main gate.	78
4.10	S. Girardo bastion: Aerial view.	79
4.11	S. Girardo bastion: Interior of the western flank.	80
4.12	S. Girardo bastion: The north screen wall and ramp.	80
4.13	S. Girardo bastion: Interior of the northern flank.	81
4.14	S. Girardo bastion: Overall view from the southeast.	82
4.15	S. Agostino bastion: Exterior of the eastern face.	84
4.16	S. Agostino bastion: Interior of the east wall.	84
4.17	S. Agostino bastion: Cistern entrance.	85
4.18	S. Agostino bastion: The main battery above the rock-cut ditch.	86
4.19	S. Agostino bastion: The interior of the gun platform.	87
4.20	S. Agostino bastion: The interior of the east postern gate and its defences.	87
4.21	S. Agostino: The exterior of the east postern gate.	88
4.22	S. Agostino: Exterior of the west postern gate.	89
4.23	S. Agostino: The defences above the west postern gate.	90
4.24	Bridge over the Arvanitia gulley.	90
4.25	Doppia Tenaglia: The west wall.	93
4.26	Doppia Tenaglia: The gun battery above the rock-cut ditch.	93
4.27	Doppia Tenaglia: Western section of gun platform.	94
4.28	Doppia Tenaglia: Arched casemates beneath the gun platform.	94
4.29	Doppia Tenaglia: The view north along the west flank.	95
4.30	Doppia Tenaglia: The postern gate.	96
4.31	Aerial view of the Turkish bastion (Fort Phokion).	98
4.32	Fort Phokion: The completed section of the planned Venetian outwork.	98

Figures

4.33	Fort Phokion: The entrance to the countermine.	99
4.34	Fort Phokion: Cistern entrance.	100
4.35	Fort Phokion: View of the exterior from the southeast.	100
4.36	Fort Phokion: The postern gate.	101
4.37	Bastione Staccato: Aerial view.	103
4.38	Bastione Staccato: Outer gate and adjacent postern.	104
4.39	Bastione Staccato: Casemates of the inner courtyard.	104
4.40	Bastione Staccato: Interior.	105
4.41	Bastione Staccato: The south flank.	106
4.42	Bastione Staccato: Detailed view of the south flank.	106
4.43	Bastione Staccato: The gun platform and upper infantry parapet of the south rampart.	107
4.44	The Piattaforma viewed from the foot of Palamidi.	109
4.45	The Piattaforma: The upper terrace.	109
4.46	The Piattaforma: The northern cistern.	110
4.47	The Piattaforma: The west face of the middle terrace.	111
4.48	Fort Epaminondas: The main gate.	113
4.49	Fort Epaminondas: Overall view from the south.	113
4.50	Fort Epaminondas: Passageway of the main gate.	114
4.51	The gun platforms and stepped parapet to the southwest of the main gate.	115
5.1	Drepanon Fort: Outer face of the sea battery.	120
5.2	Drepanon Fort: The gunpowder magazine.	120
5.3	Drepanon Fort: Gun embrasures of the sea battery.	121
6.1	Thermisi: The crags from the south.	125
6.2	Thermisi: The north wall of the outer bailey.	125
6.3	Thermisi: The walls of the inner bailey viewed from the east.	126
6.4	Thermisi: The northeast corner of the inner bailey.	127
6.5	Thermisi: The apse of the Byzantine chapel.	128
6.6	Thermisi: The inner bailey from the west.	129
6.7	Thermisi: The southwest walls of the outer bailey.	130

All photographs are by the author with the exception of Figs. 4.10, 4.31 and 4.37 which are stills taken from drone footage published by worldanddrone.eu under a Creative Commons Attribution licence.

Maps and Plans

1	The Venetian Morea	x
2	Modern Nafplio and the surviving fortifications	2
3	Byzantine Nafplio	12
4	Nafplio c. 1540	15
5	Nafplio c. 1714	21
6	The Grimani bastion	29
7	Castle of the Rock (the Bourtzi)	34
8	The eastern acropolis fortifications until the early 20C	44
9	The development of the east front of the Castle of the Franks	54
10	The Palamidi fortifications	67
11	The Maschio (Fort Robert)	70
12	Bastione S. Girardo (Fort Andreas)	76
13	Mezzo-baloardo S. Agostino (Fort Themistokles)	83
14	The Doppia Tenaglia (Fort Achilles) and Turkish bastion (Fort Phokion)	92
15	The Bastione Staccato (Fort Miltiades)	102
16	The Piattaforma (Fort Leonidas)	108
17	Fort Epaminondas and the southeast defences	112
18	Drepanon Fort	118
19	The Castle of Thermisi	124

Outline maps of Greece are based on Landsat7 images in the public domain courtesy of NASA Goddard Space Flight Centre and the U.S. Geological Survey.

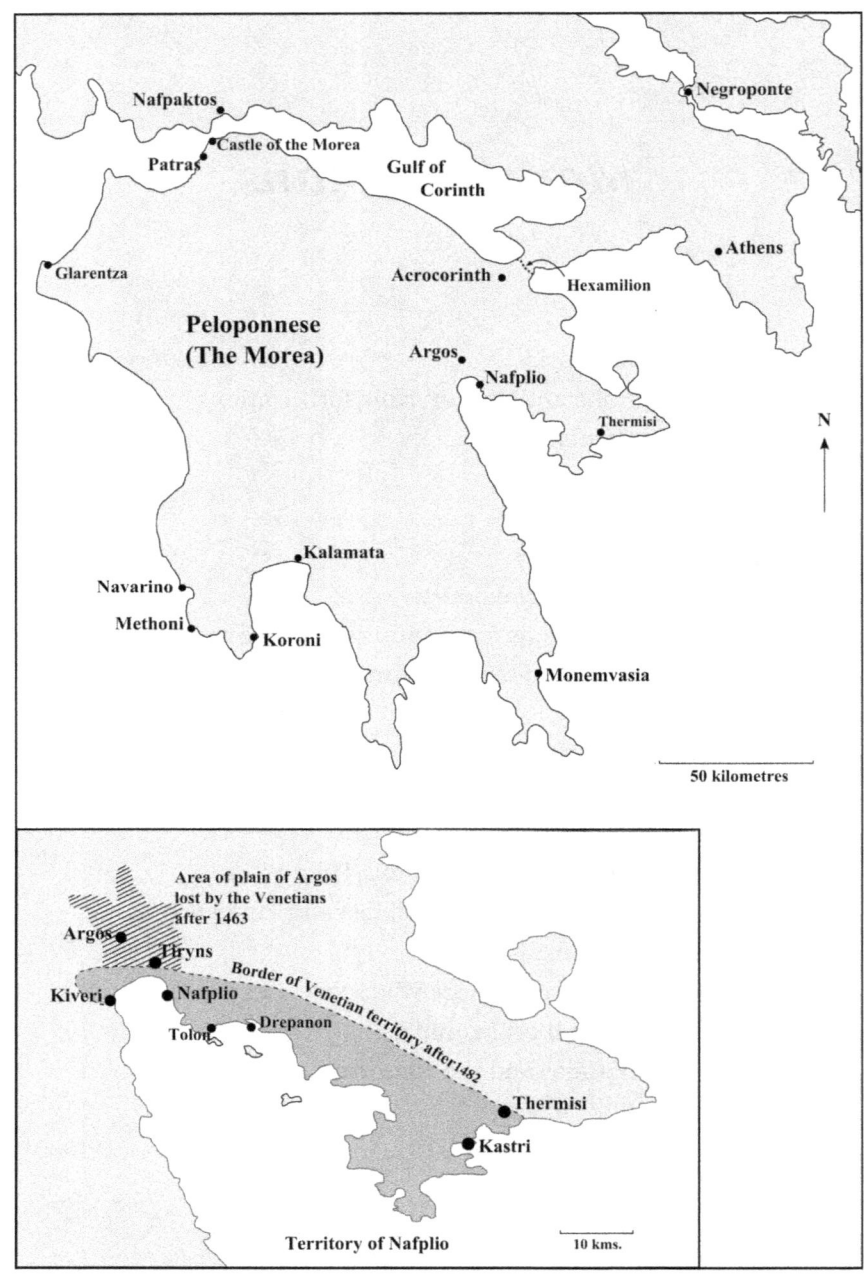

Plan 1 The Venetian Morea.

Preface

Nafplio* has been a port since antiquity and fortifications have existed on its acropolis from at least the 3C BC. Although the town was abandoned when Pausanias visited, the site was re-settled by the early Byzantine period. After the sack of Constantinople in 1204 it was first conquered by the Franks before enduring alternate periods of occupation by the Venetians and the Turks. Foreign control came to an end only in 1822.

The fortifications that still dominate the town belong primarily to the two periods of Venetian occupation although elements from other eras can still be found amongst the Venetian works. These include the lower courses of walls from the 3C BC, Byzantine towers and sections of mediaeval Frankish work. The Venetian programme of re-fortification began in the second half of the fifteenth century in response to Turkish incursions and the threat posed by improvements in gunpowder weapons. They continued to develop the defences until they were forced to cede the territory to the Turks in 1540. The Venetians returned in 1687 having wrested the entire Morea from Ottoman control. Nafplio became the capital of their new territory and the Venetians embarked on a building programme that included a substantial new bastioned front to protect the lower town and improvements to the defences of the acropolis. Their final work at Nafplio proved to be the last major fortification to be constructed anywhere by the Republic. This was the extensive and innovative system of artillery defences that still stand on the commanding heights of Palamidi high above the town to the southeast.

This book discusses the evolution of the fortifications that have defended the town and its port through the centuries. It provides a detailed guide to the substantial elements that survive and a description

---

* Nafplio is the most common transliteration of the Greek Ναύπλιον. Alternatives are: Nauplio and Navplio. To the Venetians it was Napoli di Romania.

Preface

of the sections that have been lost. The survivals include the acropolis defences, the fifteenth century Venetian fort built on a rock in the harbour entrance, sections of the first walls enclosing the lower town, fragments of the great land walls built by the Venetians between 1701 and 1711 and finally the system of fortifications atop the mountain of Palamidi. The book also describes the fortifications of the outlying territory connected to the city: the castle of Thermisi protecting the valuable salt pans on the southern coast of the Argolid and the artillery fort at Drepanon defending the entrance to an important harbour.

Access to the sites

The surviving fortifications of the lower town and the acropolis can be inspected at any time as can the castle of Thermisi and Drepanon fort.
Boats from the town quay provide access to the Bourtzi.
The Palamidi fortifications are subject to standard opening hours; usually 08.00 to 15.00 in winter, 08.00 to 19.00 in summer. There are ticket offices at the head of the stairs from the lower town and at the main entrance within Fort Epaminondas which can be reached by car.

Introduction

Nafplio lies near the head of the Gulf of Argos on its eastern side. The rocky peninsula of Acronauplia, the acropolis of the earliest settlement, projects westwards into the bay forming a sheltered anchorage to the north. Much of the peninsula is over 60m in height with near vertical cliffs to the south and west, originally falling directly into the sea. On the northern side the western cliffs give way to steep slopes that descend to the shoreline. Until the late 15C there was only a narrow strip of flat land between the acropolis slope and the shore but this has widened considerably over the centuries through a combination of the natural silting of the bay and human intervention. This level area is now occupied by the old town. The eastern end of the acropolis hill descends in series of terraces to a narrow defile that separates it from the mass of the hill of Palamidi to the southeast. This peak rises to over 200m and dominates the town. It too has high cliffs on its seaward, southwestern flank. Originally access to Nafplio from the plain to the north was via a narrow approach between the steep northern slopes of Palamidi and the marshes at the head of the bay.

   Nafplio has been settled since the early Bronze Age and evidence of Mycenaean occupation has been found. Although the place is not mentioned by Homer, Euripides does refer to Menelaos's ships riding at anchor in the harbour on his return from Troy. The city must have been of some importance by the 7C BC, when it was an ally of Sparta, but its independence was curtailed when it was destroyed by Damokratidas of Argos and its inhabitants were expelled. Thereafter it became the port for the territory of Argos and around 300 BC the acropolis was fortified. Substantial traces of these first walls can still be seen beneath the later Byzantine, Frankish and Venetian work. It was still known as the naval base of Argos in Strabo's time but by the 2C AD Pausanias described Nafplio as abandoned with its walls in ruins although he still mentions its harbours. Nafplio was re-established in the early Byzantine period possibly as a result of population shift

Introduction

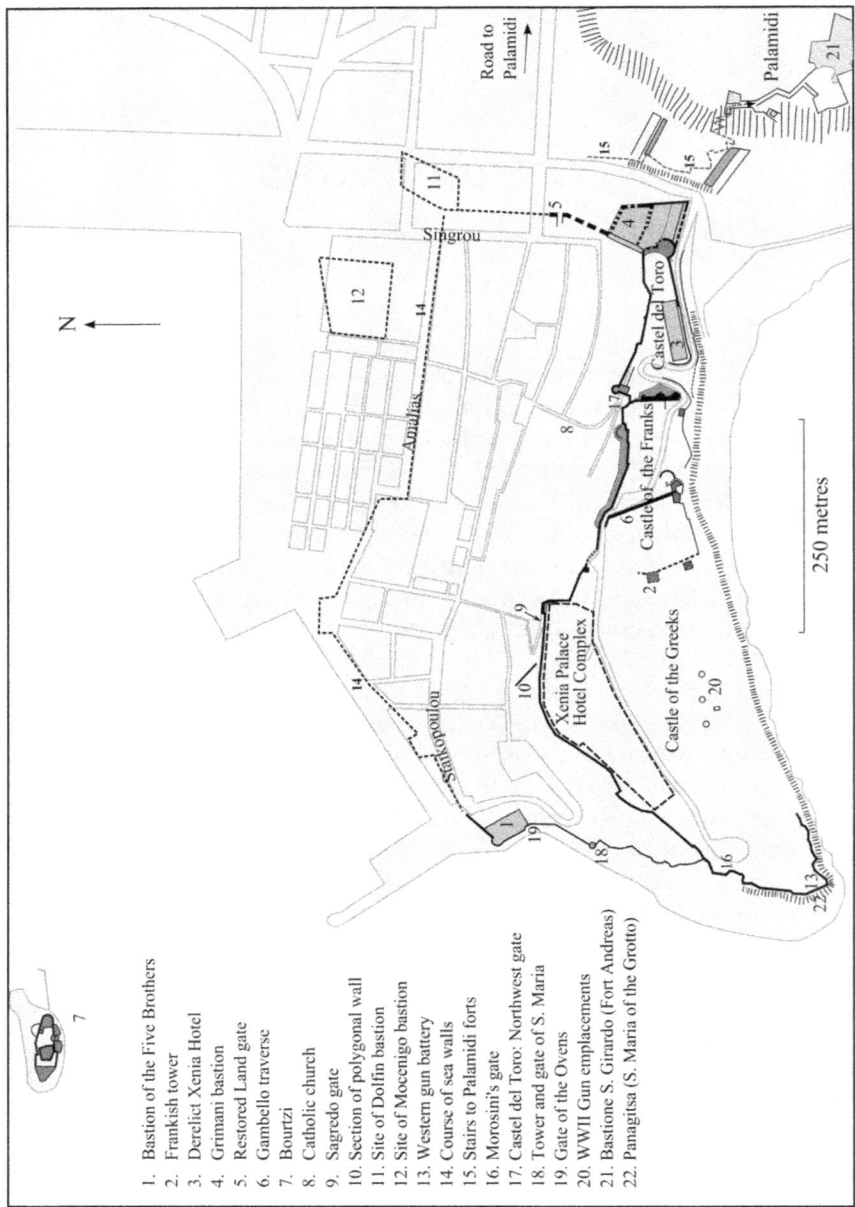

1. Bastion of the Five Brothers
2. Frankish tower
3. Derelict Xenia Hotel
4. Grimani bastion
5. Restored Land gate
6. Gambello traverse
7. Bourtzi
8. Catholic church
9. Sagredo gate
10. Section of polygonal wall
11. Site of Dolfin bastion
12. Site of Mocenigo bastion
13. Western gun battery
14. Course of sea walls
15. Stairs to Palamidi forts
16. Morosini's gate
17. Castel del Toro: Northwest gate
18. Tower and gate of S. Maria
19. Gate of the Ovens
20. WWII Gun emplacements
21. Bastione S. Girardo (Fort Andreas)
22. Panagitsa (S. Maria of the Grotto)

Plan 2 Modern Nafplio: The surviving fortifications of the acropolis and the lower town showing the line of the demolished sea walls and land front.

eastwards following Slav incursions into the Peloponnese. In subsequent centuries it appears sporadically in the historical record but it must have been of real commercial importance by 1082 when a treaty was concluded between Venice and the Byzantines. In exchange for naval assistance Venice was granted free trade rights in a long list of Byzantine towns including Nafplio.[1]

There is no record of the date at which Nafplio was refortified by the Byzantines but at some point new walls were built upon the ruins of the old. Possible dates range from the 3C to the late 12C, when, in 1180, Theodore Sgouros was appointed archon of the Nafplio area and given a Byzantine fleet to protect the coast against piracy.[2] Towards the end of the century his son, Leon, inherited the title and by 1203 he had also established control over Argos and Corinth. His expansionary policy was halted by the arrival of the Franks in mainland Greece in 1204 following the fall of Constantinople. Argos and Corinth held out against Frankish sieges until 1210. Sgouros may have died in Nafplio in 1208 but he is generally supposed to have committed suicide by riding his horse over the cliffs of Acrocorinth.[3] With the help of four Venetian galleys Geoffrey I de Villehardouin then besieged Nafplio and it fell to the Franks in 1212.[4] They occupied the acropolis and subsequently created a separate enclosure in the eastern part of the original enceinte. This became known as the Castle of the Franks. The remainder, to the west, was called the Castle of the Greeks.

Argos and Nafplio were given by Villehardouin to Otho de la Roche. He and his descendants held them from 1212 until 1308 when Guy II died without issue. Title to the territory passed to his cousin, Walter de Brienne, his son, and then by marriage to the d'Enghien family in 1356.[5] Venetian control came almost voluntarily in 1377 when Marie, the last surviving member of the d'Enghien family, sought Venetian protection and cemented the arrangement by marriage to the Venetian Pietro Cornaro.[6] When he died in 1388 Marie sold Nafplio and Argos to Venice. Before the Republic could assert control the area was seized by the Despot, Theodore. The Venetians occupied Nafplio but the remainder of the territory, Argos, Thermisi and Kiveri, did not fall into their hands until 1394.[7]

Initially the colony of Nafplio was of secondary importance to the twin ports of Methoni and Koroni in Messenia and the island of Negroponte (Euboia), Venetian possessions since the early 13C. The Venetians were slow to repair or improve the fortifications of the town despite the threat of Turkish incursions into the Morea.[8] These attacks began in 1397 when Argos was sacked and held briefly by the Turks.[9] Sultan Murad II's commander, Turahan, invaded the Morea in 1423

Introduction

and again in 1446 causing much destruction before withdrawing.[10] In 1453 Mehmet II seized Constantinople. The Venetians' initial response to this threat was to improve the fortifications of Negroponte.[11] However Mehmet's forces crossed the Isthmus of Corinth into the Morea in 1458 and by 1461 the entire peninsula, with the exception of the Venetian colonies, was in his hands.[12] Again Nafplio was ignored during 1461 and 1462 in favour of improvements to the defences of Methoni.[13] The Turks then occupied Argos in 1462 and the following year the first Venetian-Turkish war began. The Venetian counter-attack under Bertoldo D'Este was initially successful. Argos was re-taken, the Hexamilion wall across the Isthmus was re-built and Acrocorinth besieged. However during this siege D'Este was killed. The Turks advanced, the Venetians abandoned their siege and the Hexamilion, retreating to Nafplio. The Hexamilion was destroyed with the Turks taking permanent possession of Argos. The Venetians held out in Nafplio while the war continued. The Republic had limited success elsewhere, sacking Athens in 1466, but a siege of Patras was a failure and the Venetians were defeated at Kalamata.[14] Then in 1470 Negroponte fell.

At last an urgent programme of re-fortification began at Nafplio. Later the same year Vettore Pasqualigo arrived from Venice with the military engineer, Antonio Gambello, together with the resources and manpower needed to modernise the town's defences. This work was to include new fortifications on the acropolis including a third enclosure (Castel del Toro) to the east of the Castle of the Franks, a fort on a rocky islet in the harbour and new walls around the developing lower town.[15] Although much was completed over the next three years, construction slowed down as the war dragged to a close. Peace with the Turks was agreed in 1479 but agreement on the exact boundary of the reduced Venetian enclave was only reached in 1482.[16] Work on the sea and land walls of the lower town continued in a sporadic fashion until the close of the century.[17]

In 1499 the Turks began a second war with the Venetians, moving first against Lepanto (modern Nafpaktos, purchased by Venice in 1407) which fell the same year. Bayezid II then built a pair of gun forts, known as the Castle of the Morea and the Castle of Roumeli, on either side of the Gulf of Corinth at the Rio narrows, thus preventing Venetian galleys entering the Gulf. The following year Bayezid marched against Nafplio with a large army. This led to a feverish resumption of work on both the land and sea walls.[18] The attack was repelled, although Thermisi was taken briefly, and the Turks moved their forces south to besiege Methoni. The fall of Methoni to the Turks in 1500 led to the surrender of first Navarino (modern Pylos) and then Koroni. When peace was agreed in 1503 the only surviving Venetian colonies in the Peloponnese were Nafplio and Monemvasia. The peace treaty of 1503 was renewed in 1513 and again in 1521 but in 1537 Suleiman I once more declared war on Venice. In this third war Nafplio was again besieged and bombarded by Turkish cannon from the heights of Palamidi. The outlying castles of Thermisi and Kastri were taken but, despite the bombardment, Nafplio held out.[19] However in 1538 the defeat of the joint fleet of the Holy League (comprising Genoa, Venice, Spain and the Papacy) at the naval battle of Preveza forced Venice to seek peace. The terms concluded in 1540 forced the Republic to cede Nafplio and Monemvasia.

Nafplio became the Ottoman capital of the Morea and prospered as the seat of the Turkish Pasha. Although another war with Venice began in 1570 when the Turks invaded Cyprus, Nafplio, along with the rest of mainland Greece, was left largely untroubled. Even the momentous defeat of the Ottoman fleet at Lepanto in 1571 had little impact in the Morea. Nafplio did not see conflict again until 1647 when, as part of diversionary attacks during the long war for the possession of Crete, the Venetian Admiral Grimani briefly blockaded the Turkish fleet within the harbour.[20] However in 1684 Venice joined a new Holy League of the Papacy, the Holy Roman Empire and Poland in a concerted attempt to drive the Turks from southeast Europe. The Venetian contribution was to be the re-conquest of the Morea. By the summer of 1686 Venetian forces led by Francesco Morosini had recovered all the main castles in Messenia including Koroni, Methoni and Navarino. They then moved against Nafplio. Morosini's land force, led by the Swedish Field Marshal Königsmark, landed on the beach at Tolon, seven kilometres to the southeast of the town. They immediately occupied the undefended heights of Palamidi and from there they were able to bombard Acronauplia and the lower town.[21] The Turks had added little, if anything, to the town's fortifications during their long tenure yet the old Venetian defences were still capable of resisting a siege. The garrison did not surrender until the Venetian forces had defeated two Turkish relief expeditions from Argos and Corinth. By the end of 1687 the whole of the Peloponnese with the single exception of Monemvasia (taken in 1690) was in Venetian hands. Hostilities with the Turks continued elsewhere. Venetian forces recovered Lepanto and took the Castles of the Morea and Roumeli but further territorial gains were short-lived. Athens was taken in 1687 but abandoned the following year. In 1688 a campaign to recover Negroponte collapsed after four months. An attempt to take Chania on Crete

Introduction

in 1692 was also quickly abandoned. Finally in 1694 the island of Chios was seized only for it to be retaken by the Turks the following year. These setbacks left the Venetians in a weak bargaining position when a peace agreement was finally negotiated at Karlowitz in 1699. The Republic was forced to give up its conquests north of the Gulf of Corinth but its possession of the entire Morea was confirmed.[22]

Nafplio became the capital of Venice's new possession and they began a massive building programme designed both to transform the town into a worthy capital and to address the weaknesses in its defences. New barracks, magazines and warehouses were constructed both on Acronauplia and in the lower town. New churches were erected and an entire new suburb developed on reclaimed land to the north of the existing sea walls. A huge, new bastioned land front was constructed between 1702 and 1711 to protect the lower town. Finally Palamidi, the key to Nafplio's security, was fortified with an elaborate complex of artillery works built between 1711 and 1714. Yet all this effort was insufficient to prevent the Turkish re-conquest the following year. The Ottoman army, said to number between seventy thousand and a hundred thousand men supported by a large fleet, crossed the Isthmus in the summer of 1715 and besieged Acrocorinth.[23] The Venetians' weakness was a chronic lack of manpower. The entire Venetian military force in the Morea numbered only eight thousand men. The garrison at Corinth was a mere four hundred strong and capitulated after only five days.[24] The Turks moved on to Nafplio, defended by a larger force of two thousand troops.[25] Their campaign began with attacks on the outworks of the Palamidi forts. After only eight days they succeeded in creating a breach in one of these outworks. The Palamidi complex was designed to provide defence in depth. If one part of the work was taken it could be fired on from the others. However the Venetians' nerve failed with this first assault and they abandoned the entire fortress, retreating into the lower town. The Turks pursued them and the town capitulated. By the end of the summer of 1715 the Turks had retaken the entire Morea. Once again Nafplio became the Ottoman capital and the town prospered for the next few decades. However by 1770 the capital had effectively moved to Tripolitsa (modern Tripoli) and Nafplio entered a long period of decline.[26] By the time William Leake visited the town in 1806 many of the houses were in ruins, the bay had silted up and the port was filled with mud and rubbish. However he was still impressed by the grandeur of the Venetian military installations.[27]

This was the state of Nafplio when it fell to Greek forces in 1822. The town remained in Greek hands throughout the protracted strug-

Introduction

gles of the War of Independence and became the capital of the new state in 1828. It remained so until 1834 when the capital was transferred to Athens. The slow modernisation and expansion that took place in the 19C led to the progressive demolition of the Venetian walls of the lower town. The northern sea walls were largely demolished in 1867. On the eastern land front the walls between the Grimani and Dolfin bastions were removed in 1894-5 together with the monumental land gate (re-erected in the late 1990s). The wet ditch beyond the walls was also filled in at this time.[28] A second period of demolition began in 1928 with the total removal of the Dolfin bastion. The destruction of the Mocenigo bastion followed after 1932. Only the Grimani bastion now survives.[29]

After 1828 Acronauplia became a military base. Between 1829 and 1834 the old Venetian barracks were renovated and Greece's first military hospital was built within the precinct of the Castle of the Franks. In 1884 a military prison was opened on Acronauplia and this later expanded to house first ordinary criminals then, after 1935, political prisoners. The prisons were closed in 1966.[30] The character of Acronauplia had already begun to change by that date with a new emphasis on tourism. A Xenia hotel, opened in 1961, was built on the terrace of the Castel del Toro destroying much of its surviving Venetian fortifications. After 1970 virtually every other structure on Acronauplia was demolished including the prison buildings and the old military hospital. A further hotel, the Xenia Palace, was built within the precinct of the Castle of the Greeks on the site of the demolished prisons. It opened in 1979 and remains in operation.

Notes

1. Peter Lock, *The Franks in the Aegean*, pp. 137-138. However the first commercial agreement between the Venice and the Byzantine Empire dates from 992. See Diana Wright, *Bartolomeo Minio: Venetian Administration in 15th Century Nauplion*, p. 4.
2. Kevin Andrews, *Castles of the Morea*, p. 90.
3. Lock, *The Franks in the Aegean*, p. 71.
4. Harold Lurier, *Crusaders as Conquerors: the Chronicle of the Morea*, p. 155.
5. Lock, *The Franks in the Aegean*, pp. 88 and 104.
6. Andrews, *Castles of the Morea*, p. 91.
7. Andrews, *Castles of the Morea*, pp. 91-92, William Miller, *Latins in the Levant*, pp. 339-342. The territory of Nafplio and Argos en-

Introduction

compassed the plain of Argos and the western side of the Argolid peninsula as far as Thermisi. Although the still imposing castle of Argos was in Venetian hands from 1394 to 1463 and again from 1686 to 1715 it was never of strategic importance to the Republic and its fabric shows no trace of these two periods of occupation. See Andrews, *Castles of the Morea*, pp. 106 to 115. The castle of Thermisi survives and is described in Chapter 6. Kiveri lay at the western end of the bay of Nafplio. The ruins of its Frankish castle still stand on the summit of a hill above the modern seaside village of Myloi, the site of ancient Lerna. The castle guarded the approach to the plain of Argos from the south. See Wallace E. Mcleod, *Kiveri and Thermisi*, pp. 378-386.

8. Guiseppe Gerola, *Le Fortificazioni di Napoli di Romania*, p. 355.
9. William Miller, *Latins in the Levant*, p. 358.
10. Miller, *Latins in the Levant*, pp. 397 and 412-414.
11. Simon Pepper, *Fortress and Fleet: The Defence of Venice's Mainland Greek Colonies in the Late Fifteenth Century*, p 30.
12. Miller, *Latins in the Levant*, p. 432ff.
13. Pepper, *Fortress and Fleet*, p. 34.
14. Miller, *Latins in the Levant*, pp. 465-470.
15. Gerola, *Fortificazioni*, p. 356.
16. The new border ran in an arc around the bay of Nafplio from Kiveri in the west to Thermisi excluding the greater part of the plain of Argos. The Frankish castle of Kiveri was abandoned at this time and a tower on the shore below seems to have taken over the function of border post. The base of the tower can still be seen built into a WWII gun emplacement. See Diana Wright and John Melville Jones, *The Greek Correspondence of Bartolomeo Minio Volume 1: Dispacci from Nauplion*, pp. 239-243.
17. When Bartolomeo Minio arrived in Nafplio in November 1479 as provveditor he reported that the construction work was in poor condition, that neither the land walls nor the sea walls were complete as had been thought, and that the work could not be finished in the absence of anyone with the knowledge of how to build foundations on piles. See Diana Wright and John Melville Jones, *Dispacci from Nauplion, 1479-1483*, pp. 5-9.

    Eventually Minio was able to complete a substantial part of the sea walls but work was still in progress in the first decade of the next century. See Gerola, *Fortificazioni*, pp. 372-373.
18. Gerola states that work proceeded day and night and that even provveditor Marzo Zen took part in the construction work. *Fortificazioni*, p. 373.

19. Miller, *Latins in the Levant*, p. 507.
20. William Miller, *Essays on the Latin Orient*, p. 383.
21. George Finlay, *The History of Greece under Othoman and Venetian Domination*, p. 217.
22. The treaty established the border of Venice's new realm at the western end of the Isthmus of Corinth. The Venetian negotiator at Karlowitz, Carlo Ruzzini had attempted, without success, to establish a more defensible border to the east of the Isthmus beyond the pass of Megara. See Peter Topping, *Venice's Last Imperial Venture*, p. 163.
23. The Venetians went to considerable effort and expense to fortify their new border and overcome its weaknesses. They rebuilt the Castle of the Morea on the southern shore of the Gulf of Corinth at the Rio narrows in an attempt to control naval access from the west. They restored and extended the fortifications of Acrocorinth intending it to house a garrison that could be deployed to defend the Isthmus. Remarkably they also attempted to build a new land barrier to invasion both north and east of Acrocorinth. To the north they built a line of earthworks between the foot of the plateau of ancient Corinth and the coast. To the east they planned further earthworks to deny the route between Acrocorinth and Mount Oneion. The passes through the ridge of the mountain were blocked with simple walls and towers. Little of the earthworks that were completed survives, although the masonry walls of Oneion still exist. See Antoine Bon, *The Medieval Fortifications of Acrocorith and Vicinity*, pp. 268-271, and William R. Caraher and Timothy E. Gregory, *Fortifications of Mount Oneion, Corinthia*, pp. 347-354.
24. Finlay, *History of Greece*, pp. 265-266.
25. Andrews, *Castles of the Morea*, p. 105, gives the total garrison in Nafplio as 1,269.
26. William Miller, *The Turkish Restoration in Greece, 1718 - 1797*, p. 29. He states that Tripolitsa formally became the capital in 1786.
27. W.M. Leake, *Travels in the Morea, Vol.II*, p. 359. Leake also gives 1790 as the date when Tripolitsa became the capital.
28. Α. Βασιλείου and Κ. Μπουντούρης, *Ναυπλιο: Σημείωμα για την εξέλιξη της πόλης*.
29. Alexander Zäh, *Venezianische Baugeschichte von Nauplia 1685-1715*, p. 144.
30. Αντωνιάδης Μπάμπης, «*Ημερολόγια*» *φυλακών της πόλης του Ναυπλίου*.

1

The Lower Town

The development of the fortifications

Today the port of Nafplio has extensive concrete quays providing deep water berths, kept accessible by dredging, with the whole harbour area protected by a long breakwater. It typifies the modern definition of a port. However in the mediaeval period, as in antiquity, artificial ports were the exception rather than the rule. A port was typically a natural location rather than a man-made construction. The first requirement for such a port was a sandy beach for loading and unloading. The second was a protecting promontory, capable of being fortified against attack, to provide shelter from winds and currents.[1] The early topography of Nafplio clearly matched this description closely and it must have been the obvious location for a port serving the large agricultural plain of Argos.

When the acropolis at Nafplio was first fortified in the 3C BC the shoreline ran along the base of the northern slope of the promontory. The early settlement lay within the acropolis walls but warehouses and workshops must have existed by the shore. There is evidence that east and west walls may have run north from the acropolis to enclose the port area. A section of such a wall is visible a few metres to the west of the base of the steps to the Sagredo gate (Plan 2, 10). Built in the same polygonal masonry as the first acropolis circuit, the surviving section runs for thirty metres in a northwesterly direction from the foot of the acropolis cliff. Traces of an eastern counterpart may have been observed by Schaefer on the western side of the road leading up to the northwest gate to Castel del Toro, above the Catholic church.[2] Whilst this early port perhaps consisted simply of the anchorage in the bay and the beach itself, it is possible that it was also protected by one or more moles. Such a mole was discovered in 1899 during the construction of a new quay projecting into the harbour.[3] This substantial structure, 250m long and five to ten metres wide, was buried in the mud

The lower town

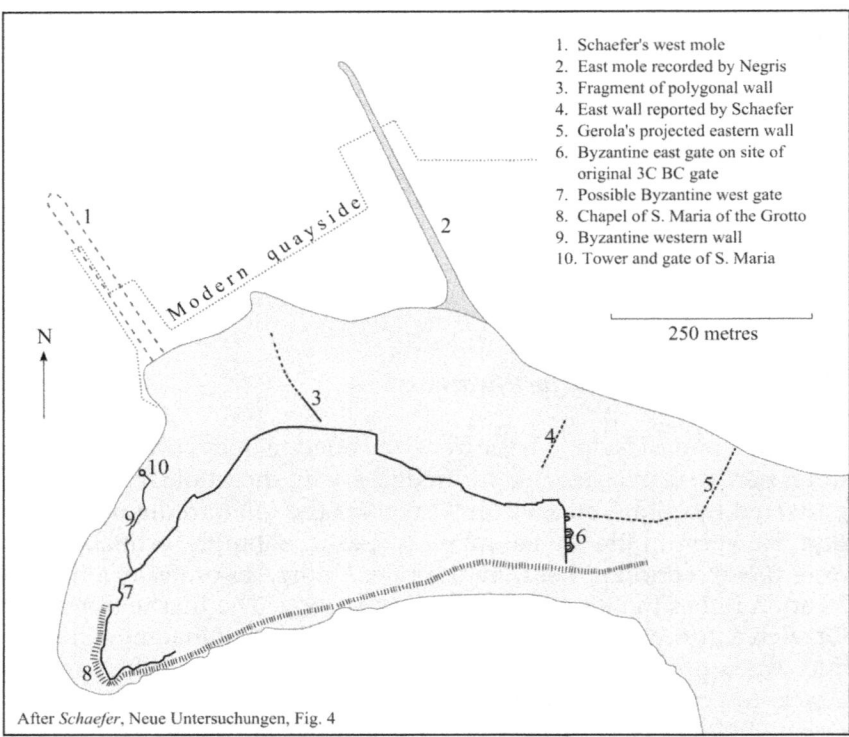

Plan 3 Byzantine Nafplio.

of the bay where the water was a mere 1.6m deep. Negris recorded that it was built of "natural blocks" up to half a cubic metre in size, and that it was not possible to assign a construction date. The inner part of the mole is presumably buried within the modern quays while the outer part was largely removed when the port was dredged to a depth of 5.5m. Located at the eastern, inner side of the port, the construction of such a mole may represent an attempt to reduce the flow of silt into the harbour area.[4] If this was the intention it was clearly unsuccessful in the long run as the mud of the bay was level with the upper surface of the mole when it was discovered.

The re-establishment of Nafplio in the Byzantine period involved both the refortification of the acropolis and the commercial area below. The western arm of these lower defences, much rebuilt, still survives and descends from the northwest corner of the acropolis to the shore (Plan 3, 9).[5] Both Schaefer and Gerola suggested that this western wall had an eastern counterpart. Schaefer alludes to evidence that

The lower town

Fig. 1.1 The polygonal wall running from the base of the acropolis cliff, exposed beneath modern terracing.

such a wall ran directly to the shore from the eastern end of the acropolis walls near the Catholic church.[6] Gerola however theorises that a Byzantine eastern wall followed the line now occupied by the north wall of Castel del Toro before descending to the sea possibly along the same course as the later Venetian land walls.[7]

The Franks besieged Nafplio at the beginning of the 13C by land and, with the assistance of four Venetian galleys, by sea. They regarded Nafplio as one of the best harbours of the Morea.[8] Although they occupied the acropolis and created the two enclosures mentioned above, it is not known whether they maintained or developed the port. The Franks were certainly capable of such engineering. The main harbour of the Principality of Achaia, as the Frankish Morea was known, was on the northwest coast at Glarentza on the strategic trade route to Italy. Here they developed a port with an excavated basin protected by moles and breakwaters built on the remains of its classical predecessor.[9] Nevertheless Nafplio must have continued as the export point for the produce of the Argolid throughout the period of the Frankokratia utilising whatever facilities were available.

When the Venetians first took possession of the town at the end of the 14C the shoreline still ran along the base of the slope below the acropolis hill and access to the town was along a narrow strip of land between the heights of Palamidi and an extensive area of marsh to the north. The surviving fortifications on the acropolis continued to be known as the Castle of the Greeks and the Castle of the Franks but their walls and towers were in poor condition. The first mention of the defences of the lower port area occur at the beginning of the 15C. Venice sent materials for their repair as early as 1401.[10] In 1404 reference is made to a ruined tower known as Sombolo, or Strombolo, on the edge of the marsh at the eastern end of the port. The same report appears to state that this tower was attached to ruined walls and a gate.[11] This presumably represented the remains of an earlier, eastern lower town wall pre-dating the Venetian occupation. Small sums were expended on various repairs throughout the first half of the 15C and the ruined tower of Strombolo was replaced by another named the Contarina tower.[12] However despite recurring pleas to Venice for funds and assistance, the defences of both the acropolis and the slowly developing lower town were otherwise neglected until Pasqualigo and Gambello arrived in Nafplio in 1470.

Pasqualigo's brief was nothing less than the complete refortification of the acropolis and the lower town. For the first time the port itself was also to be protected by building a sea fort on the small island or reef standing in the bay some 500m offshore (see Chapter 2). Entrance to the port was between this island and the shore as the bay north of the island was too shallow for the passage of vessels. The new works would narrow this approach and it would be defended by gun batteries on the sea fort with another battery on the shore opposite on the site of the bastion of the Five Brothers.[13] In addition the island would be encircled and protected by a submerged stone barrier. This *porporella* was meant to be concealed just below the surface of the water. It would both control access to the island itself and, together with a mole extending from the shore, greatly narrow the harbour entrance restricting the possible force of a sea-borne attack. The lower town was then to be enclosed with a sea wall running from the Contarina tower westwards to meet the old Byzantine wall descending from Acronauplia to the shore. Finally a rebuilt eastern, or land, wall and gate would connect the Contarina tower with the new enclosure of Castel del Toro on the acropolis. These new walls would increase the area of the lower town substantially but would involve reclaiming a large area of salt marsh. Over the next three years the bulk of the work planned on the acropolis was completed, as was the sea fort, although much was subsequently updated or had to be repaired later in the century. However the porporella itself was not completed, leaving the new fort unnecessarily exposed to attack.[14] Only fractions of the

The lower town

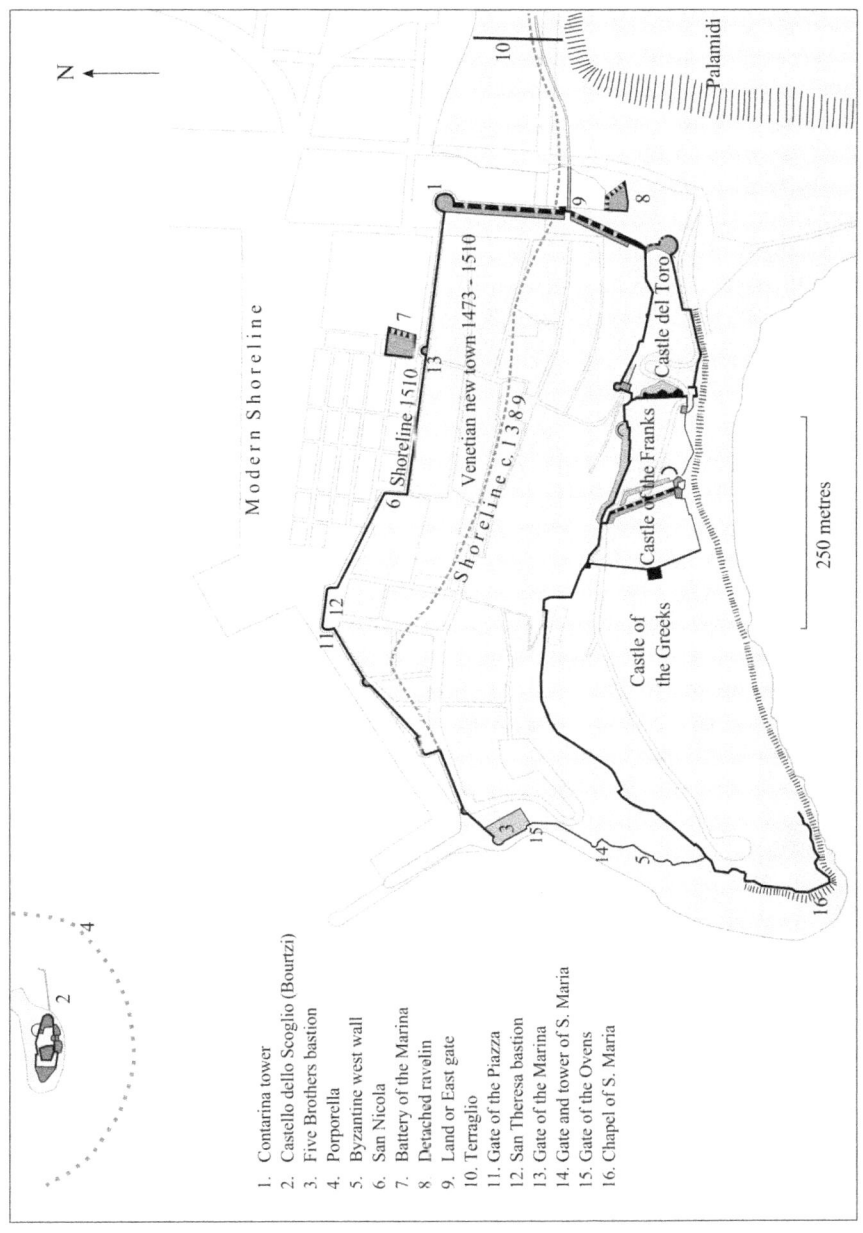

Plan 4 Nafplio c. 1540 superimposed on the modern street plan.
Derived from *Schaefer*, Neue Untersuchungen, Fig. 1.

The lower town

planned land front and sea wall were actually built during Pasqualigo's three year tenure. Perhaps it was inevitable that such an ambitious project would only be partially completed. Nevertheless the plan of the lower town circuit that he began determined its layout for the next two hundred years.

When Bartolomeo Minio arrived as provveditor in 1479 he discovered that the greatest obstacle to completion of the sea walls was the need to build on marshland and that Nafplio possessed no one with the necessary skill to construct foundations on piles.[15] Minio also found that only half the projected land front had been completed. In fact the principal defence of the lower town was an advance earthwork running from the base of the Palamidi rock the short distance to the marsh. By the end of his tenure in 1483 Minio had rebuilt this *terraglio* in stone and also completed the sea walls from the west as far as the church of S Nicolo.[16] However the necessary piling for the remaining section up to the Contarina tower was not put in place until 1499. The sea walls and the eastern land front were only finally completed in the first decades of the 16C.[17] A entire new suburb was created within these new walls. When the project was finished the land front projected east in a shallow V-shape with a square tower at its apex containing the land or east gate. Beyond the wall was an outer wet ditch open to the sea to the north. A detached work, or ravelin, stood at the head of the ditch below Castel del Toro with a gun battery facing north to enfilade the wall and gate.[18] The main sea gate, the gate of the Marina, was halfway between the Contarina tower and S. Nicolo. It was protected by a stone outwork on the beach, known as the battery of the Marina, equipped with three or four guns facing east. The rampart of the land front itself seems to have been furnished with embrasures. The all important porporella was not completed until 1515.[19] The defences were now strong enough to resist Suleiman's bombardment in 1537 but were of no avail when the treaty ending the third Ottoman-Venetian war ceded Nafplio to the Turks in 1540.

Throughout the period of the first Venetian occupation Nafplio was a port of call and a harbour of refuge rather than a naval base. The Republic needed to maintain a network of such ports as galleys had both a limited range and poor sea-keeping abilities in bad weather. Their low freeboard meant that they were forced to seek shelter when the weather deteriorated. Two weeks was regarded as the maximum time they could stay at sea before they had to replenish supplies.[20] Oared galleys needed to carry abundant water for their crews and a good supply of fresh water was an essential requirement for any port. Nafplio provided both a sheltered anchorage and an excellent supply of water; an aqueduct had brought water into the city from the springs near Aria since the beginning of the 15C.[21] However as a port it was otherwise notable for its lack of facilities. Silting must have been a continual problem. The inner port was shallow and marshy and, although Nafplio was an export point, goods were normally shipped in smaller craft to Methoni for transhipment to larger galleys.[22] There were no facilities for making repairs to vessels. Bartolomeo Minio's Dispacci give two examples of these limitations. In 1482 a galley put into Nafplio with storm damage and its captain was left to repair it as best he could in the absence of any facilities in the port.[23] Later in 1482 a force of seven galleys arrived in response to Turkish naval attacks. Two of the vessels required repairs and this could only be done by careening the hulls on the beach of Karathonas to the south of the Nafplio headland.[24]

The Turks held Nafplio for almost one hundred and fifty years, from 1540 until 1686. Although they had a considerable impact on the appearance and architecture of the town, their contributions were limited to the erection of public buildings, baths, fountains and mosques. They left the fortifications unchanged although they must have kept them in repair as they were still capable of resisting Morosini's siege. The Venetian re-conquest illustrated dramatically the weakness of these defences in an era of powerful gunpowder weapons. As a port Nafplio had to be defended from naval attack but equally it had to be protected on the landward side. Here it was now vulnerable to the artillery of the day. Not only was much of the acropolis and the lower town overlooked from the hill of Palamidi, but the approaches to these heights from the east were easily accessible and undefended. There were several good landing sites for land forces to be found on beaches to the southeast. When Morosini's forces landed on such a beach at Tolon in 1686, they occupied Palamidi without opposition and were able to bombard the town with impunity. Nafplio was in Venetian hands by the end of 1686. However hostilities with the Turks continued and stability did not return to the area until the Treaty of Karlowitz was signed in January 1699. The Venetians' first project in their new dominion was to survey the surviving fortifications and produce a full census of the territory. This survey produced the drawings known as the Grimani plans.[25] At Nafplio a scheme was drawn up to modernise the fortifications and address the weaknesses revealed by Morosini's siege. The land front was to be rebuilt on a massive scale. The first proposal involved a straight curtain wall flanked by bastions, one on the site of the Contarina tower and another below Castel del Toro beyond the end of the wet ditch. At the mid-point of the wall would be a new monumental gate.[26] Although an overall plan was drawn up by Cittadella with the engineers Levasseur and LaSalle, work actually proceeded in a sporadic fashion between 1702 and 1711 and the first design was subsequently modified.

The first element to be built was the S. Marco, or Dolfin, bastion named after Daniele Dolfin IV, governor from 1701 to 1704. This replaced, or more probably enveloped, the existing Contarina tower. Work began in 1702 and the bastion was complete by 1704. It was designed to flank the land walls and gate, seal off the seaward end of the line and protect the approach to the town from the east which ran between the northern slope of Palamidi and the marsh. When first completed the sea and the wet ditch reached all four faces of the bastion but the continuing problem of silting meant that it was quickly surrounded by a new beach. The loss of the bastion's water defences created a weakness which was eventually addressed by the construction of a detached island bastion in the bay to the northwest. Although planned as early as 1706, it was not completed until 1711. Known as the Mocenigo bastion after Alvise Mocenigo, Grimani's successor, it was approximately twice the size of the Dolfin bastion.[27] Its construction involved the demolition of the old battery of the Marina in 1709. A small harbour basin was created on the new bastion's inner, southern side and in 1713 an arsenal building was constructed within its walls to store replacement masts for ships and galleys.[28]

Work on the remainder of the land front started in 1706. The original scheme to straighten the curtain wall was abandoned as it would have involved the demolition of the garrison's barracks. The new wall was rebuilt in a similar fashion to its predecessor and simply followed the existing shallow V-shape with the land gate at the apex as before.[29] As a result, the proposed southern work, the San Antonio or Grimani bastion, had to be increased in size to ensure it still provided adequate flanking fire down the length of the curtain. Built partly around the base of Castel del Toro and partly against the old land wall, this massive bastion was constructed in three tiers ascending the hill beyond the southern end of the moat. The north faces of the two lower tiers housed deep gun embrasures covering the length of the land front. The upper tier formed a south facing rampart with embrasures commanding the beach of Arvanitia below. The moat was also re-modelled and widened. South of the moat a dry ditch was cut into the slope of the hill around the Grimani bastion. Although these works greatly improved the defences of the land approach to the town, the new Grimani bastion was itself overlooked by the lower slopes of Palamidi less than thirty metres to the east at the narrowest point. In an attempt to

The lower town

Fig. 1.2 The overgrown remains of the three-tiered Grimani bastion built against the eastern face of Castel del Toro.

Fig. 1.3 The stepped caponier beneath the rocks of Palamidi.

prevent access to these slopes, particularly from the south, two flanking works were constructed on the rocky hillside opposite each corner of the Grimani bastion. The northern work (Plan 5, 8) consists of a low infantry rampart facing north protected by a rock cut ditch with a walled counterscarp. The southern work (Plan 5, 9) is a long, vaulted caponier that rises in stepped sections up the hillside. Numerous loopholes for small arms pierce its thick walls and it is reinforced with another deep rock cut ditch on its southern side.[30] Enfilading fire could be directed down the length of this ditch from the parapet of a terrace cut into the rocks at its head.[31] None of these works, however, addressed the fundamental weakness of Nafplio's position; the need to control the heights of Palamidi itself. Plans to fortify the mountain had been continuously deferred as too expensive since the Venetians' arrival, but eventually in 1711 work started and by 1714 the complex of forts that survives virtually intact today was complete.

Nafplio was finally transformed into a naval base during the years of the second Venetian occupation, particularly after 1700. Although the port had still been capable of sheltering a Turkish fleet in 1647 (see above) by the time of Morosini's arrival in 1686 the harbour was badly silted up. In fact one of Morosini's first acts after taking possession of the town was to build steps from a gate at the western end of Acronauplia (Plan 5, 18) down to the shoreline, presumably to provide more direct access to a deep water anchorage off the tip of the peninsula.[32] The situation was no better in 1701 when Francesco Grimani reported that the harbour would be unusable if not dredged. One of the Grimani plans, dating from perhaps 1700, shows a proposal for dredging a narrow channel along the length of the sea walls from the harbour entrance.[33] The Venetians certainly had the technology to dredge the bed of a port; specialist machines were in use in Venice itself as early as 1545.[34] Such a channel must have been created some time in the next decade as by 1711 a small harbour basin had been constructed between the Mocenigo bastion and the shore. By 1713 the arsenal building within its walls had been erected. Two galleys were discovered here around 1932 when the bastion was being demolished.[35] Buried in the mud of the basin they may have lain in this position since 1715. The silted state of the harbour in 1700 would also account for the position of a new water source, the Cistern of the Port, erected in that year at the western end of the sea walls close to the harbour entrance. This cistern was connected to the main public aqueduct. Its massive four aisled structure survived until 1932.

Despite these improvements Nafplio still had limitations as a naval base. In particular it lacked any dry dock facilities for the repair of

The lower town

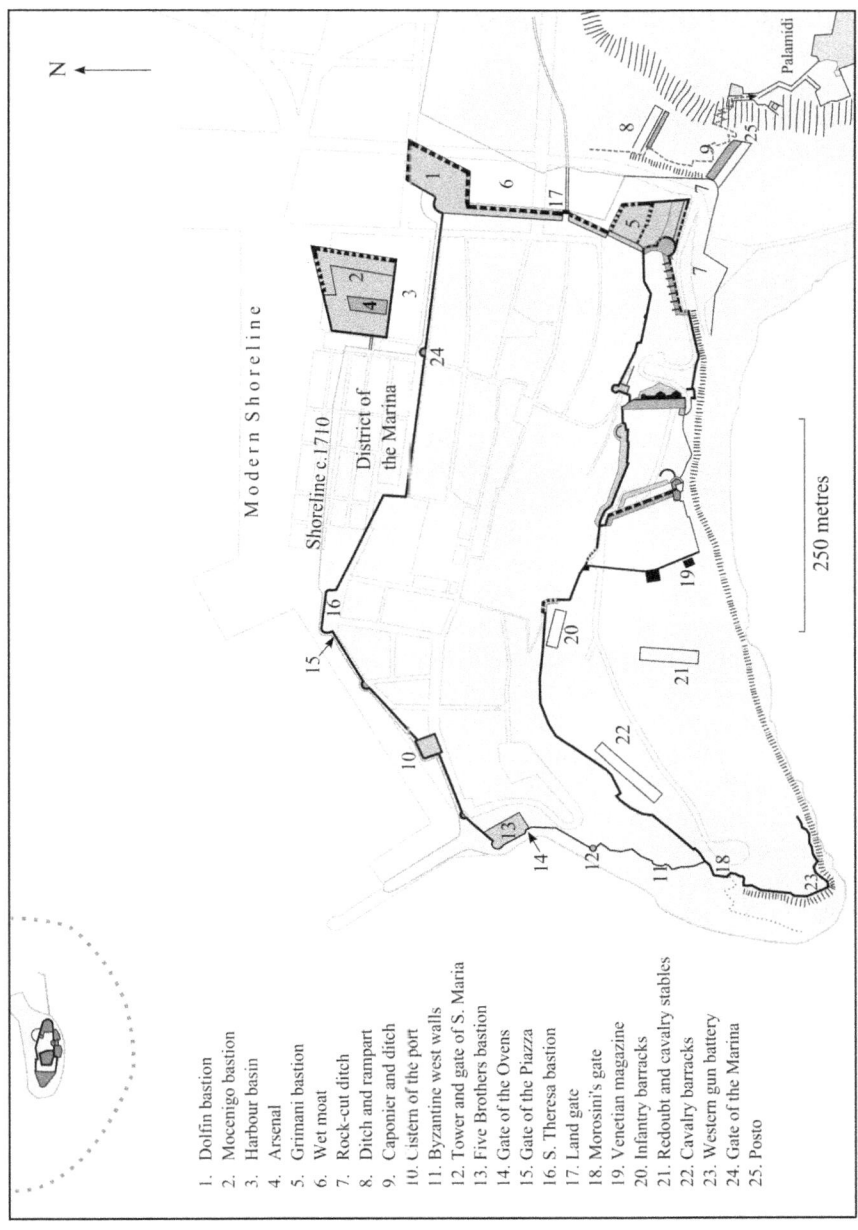

Plan 5 Nafplio c. 1714 superimposed on the modern street plan.
Derived from *Schaefer*, Neue Untersuchungen, Figs. 1 and 3.

the fleet. The Venetians seem to have used the long, almost land-locked bay of Drepanon about twelve kilometres southeast of Nafplio for this repair work (see chapter 5). The importance of this anchorage was such that a gun battery was built in 1714 to defend the entrance to the bay.[36]

The town walls today

The only surviving part of the town walls which may pre-date the first Venetian occupation is the long northwest segment that runs diagonally down the slopes of the hill from the western end of the acropolis circuit to the shore. The best description is still that of Kevin Andrews. "This is a thin wall, built with a diversity of rubble, which offers little clue to periods or builders. Certain sections are full of tile chips. Others are made of big, sharp stones, held in a strong mortar, with carefully fitted blocks in the angles." There are also repairs from the second Venetian period where Andrews notes the use of thick, yellow, Venetian bricks.[37] The wall ends at a tall, round tower with a slight batter that must originally have stood at the water's edge. A modern path raised some two metres above sea level now stands between the tower and the sea. The tower is constructed of rough rubble masonry but lacks the typical Venetian cordon and must predate the adjoining stretch of wall running north to the Five Brothers bastion. Evidence for its early date is the inverted keyhole gun port near the base.[38] Gerola refers to materials being sent from Venice to update the tower of S. Maria in 1401.[39] It is tempting to speculate that the gun port may date from this year. The tower's parapet, however, is much rebuilt and now has one arched and two open gun embrasures. The tower flanks a long blocked-up gate on its southern side that must have been sited to provide access to the chapel of S. Maria of the Grotto (now the Panagitsa) at the tip of the peninsula. The opening of the gate is well above ground level and the steps that gave access have disappeared. Maps from the 16C show that a short moat, or inlet from the sea, lay in front of the gate with access via a bridge. Vittorio Diedo in 1531 calls it the Gate of the Grotto and refers to its use as a landing place due to the silting up of the inner harbour.[40] Although the tower must originally have been hollow, its interior, as well as the entire area inside the gate, is now infilled and occupied by derelict modern concrete structures.

The wall running north from this point and the Five Brothers bastion itself were probably amongst the works completed by Pasqualigo after 1470. Above the distinctive cordon the parapet has clearly been

The lower town

Fig. 1.4 The Venetian wall between the Five Brothers bastion and the tower of S. Maria to the right. The keyhole gun port (inset) is located at the base of the tower close to the wall.

Fig 1.5. The walled-up gate of the Grotto.

repaired many times and its splayed embrasures may be late Venetian or Turkish rebuilding. The bastion has a broad gun platform equipped with five gun positions from which its name derives. Five 17C Venetian artillery pieces are now displayed in position. The 16C Gate of the Ovens (Porta dei Forni) pierces the wall by the southern flank of the bastion and leads up to the gun platform by a vaulted and stepped passage. Gerola believed that the name of the Five Brothers is of Turkish origin and speculated that in its current form the work itself may

Fig. 1.6 The interior of the gate of the Ovens.

The lower town

Fig. 1.7 Section of the foundations of the sea wall.

be Turkish. The outline of the bastion does suggest that an earlier round tower may have been absorbed into a later larger work.

The seafront to the north of the Five Brothers is now occupied by a broad modern quay built on top of the Venetian mole that extended towards the Bourtzi, the sea fort known to the Venetians as the Castello dello Scoglio, the Castle of the Rock. From the Five Brothers bastion the walls turn northeast and then disappear beneath a modern road (Staikopoulou). The line continues on the southern side of the wide modern esplanade passing the site of the Cistern of the Port, demolished in 1932. Roughly in front of the Hotel Grand Bretagne stood the S. Theresa bastion with the Gate of the Piazza in the angle of its western flank. From this point eastwards the course of the wall is preserved in the modern street plan. The broad street of Amalias was created when the walls were demolished in 1867. Their foundations still exist directly below the surface on the southern side of this street and were last revealed in 2013 during resurfacing work. A short section has been consolidated and left visible at the western end of the street. To the south of Amalias is the area of the Venetian lower town that developed after 1473 on reclaimed land. To the north is another

Fig. 1.8 The restored land gate. A short section of the bridge over the moat has been recreated. Originally this section would have lifted. The slots through which lifting chains would have run can be seen on either side of the arch.

Venetian creation, the district of the Marina, built on a grid pattern between 1706 and 1715 on more reclaimed land to the west of the Mocenigo bastion.[41] The long northern sea wall ended at the Contarina tower. Its foundations now lie beneath the paved surface of the Plateia of Kapodistrias, an open area created when the Dolfin bastion was demolished. Opposite, the town's high school stands on the site of the Mocenigo bastion. From this point the walls ran south to the land gate. The squares and open spaces to the east of Singrou street occupy the area of the demolished walls and the infilled moat beyond. The outer façade of the land gate (Fig. 1.8) however was rebuilt in the late 1990s from surviving drawings and descriptions.[42] The mutilated carving of a lion above the gate is original. Presumably a vaulted corridor led from the outer gate through the thickness of the wall. The rebuilt stub walls on the inner side of gate indicate the original thickness. The lower courses of the short stretch of curtain wall from the gate to the Grimani bastion are exposed. A timber bridge led across the wet ditch to the gate. A short section of the bridge has been re-created and the moat has been partially excavated from the gate to its southern limit at the base of the Grimani bastion. The stone revetments that formed the edge of the ditch have been revealed.

The quadrangular Grimani bastion survives largely intact and old photographs show that its appearance and construction were typical of the land front as a whole. However, while the Dolfin and Mocenigo bastions were built on level ground, the Grimani bastion stands on the slope of the low shoulder connecting the heights of Palamidi to the acropolis hill and is built in three rising terraces. The Venetians clearly intended their new defences to be physically imposing and the north face of the lower terrace is carefully built of ashlar blocks. For the lower two-thirds of the wall, some eleven courses, the blocks are heavily rusticated. The remaining five courses up to the heavy cordon are smooth faced. The brick built parapet above the cordon is now largely

Fig. 1.9 Grimani bastion: The north face. The stone revetments of the excavated moat can be seen in the foreground.

The lower town

destroyed but is it is still possible to distinguish four of the gun embrasures. In the centre of the wall is a relief of the Venetian lion within a frame embossed with three instances of the Grimani arms. Below is a separate, smaller plaque with Grimani's initials and the date 1706. A brick built sentry box corbelled out from the northeast corner survives. The construction of rusticated blocks below smooth ashlar continues for a few metres around this corner but the greater part of the stepped east face is built of roughly coursed irregular blocks, heavily mortared. Another massive lion relief adorns this face. For a few metres either side of the southeast corner the construction is again smooth ashlar above heavily rusticated blocks but this reverts to roughly coursed masonry for the greater part of the south face which runs tangentially into the curve of the great round bastion of Castel del Toro.

The dry ditch which was cut around the east and south faces of the Grimani bastion is now occupied by the modern road up to Acronauplia. To the south the counterscarp continued beneath the wall of Castel del Toro where the ditch finally opened onto the beach. These features have now all disappeared beneath modern roads, car parks and tourist installations. Tunnel vaulted internal galleries run within the

Fig. 1.10 Grimani bastion: The interior below Castel del Toro. To the right is the door opening onto the second terrace from the walled corridor. In the centre are the steps to the door cut into the face of the round tower.

The lower town

north, east and south sides of the bastion at various levels allowing movement around the work under cover. Two sally ports gave access into the ditch from the galleries. The northeast, lower entrance is a square opening at the foot of the long east face. It opens into a gallery running uphill to the southeast corner of the bastion where there is another square opening in the south face. The southern gallery runs the length of the wall climbing the full height of the rampart to an opening behind the parapet beneath the round tower of Toro. The sally ports must have been equipped with gates but they are now open and allow access to the interior of bastion. This is easiest from the northeast entrance where an opening in the west wall of the ascending gallery leads onto the overgrown lower terrace of the bastion below the parapet. From this point the well preserved brick wall that revets the second terrace can be seen. The cordon of this wall survives as do a few courses of the brick parapet above. This was the bastion's most powerful battery with seven deep gun embrasures.

The western side of the bastion is built hard against the 15C land wall and its completion made the parapet of this earlier wall redundant. The parapet was demolished and replaced by a walled passage

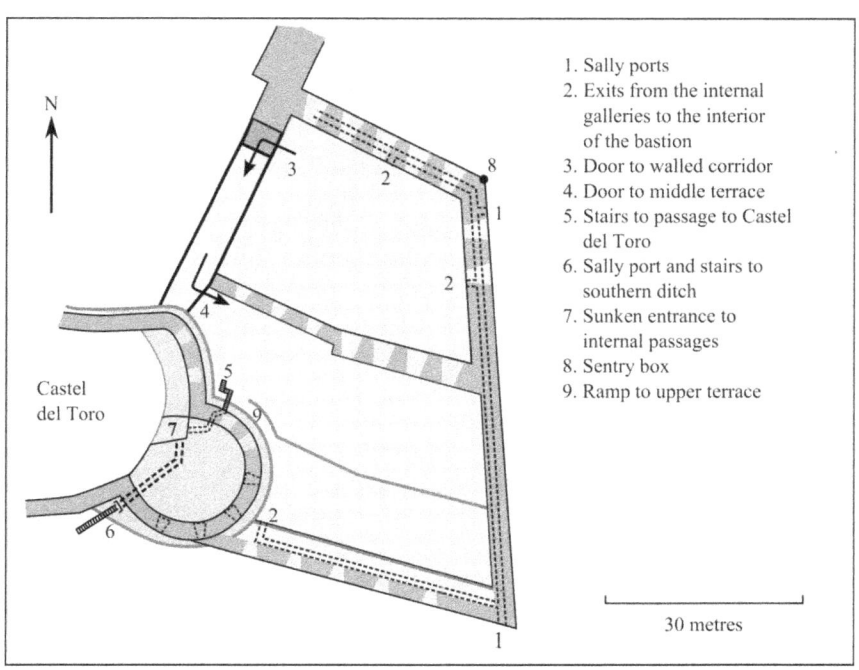

Plan 6 The Grimani bastion showing the internal galleries.

running along the top of the old wall above the level of the original cordon which can still be seen at the base of the exterior face of the east wall of the passage. At the northwest corner of the bastion a square doorway with a relieving arch above leads from the lower terrace into a small, square, vaulted chamber. Ahead is an identical door that now opens onto an unprotected vertical drop into Singrou street below. Traces of steps at street level indicate the original means of access. An arched doorway to the left leads into the walled passage which climbs to the foot of Castel del Toro. At the head of the corridor another arched door in the east wall gives access to the middle terrace behind its parapet. Steep steps built against the heavily battered walls of the great circular bastion of Castel del Toro climb to a door set halfway up the tower. From this door a passageway, cut through the 15C masonry when the Grimani bastion was built, provides a route between the new defences and the earlier enclosure of Toro.[43] Beyond the base of the steps a ramp curves around the foot of the tower and gives access to the bastion's upper terrace and the southern rampart, now ruined and overgrown.

Notes

1. Myrto Veikou, *Mediterranean Byzantine Ports and Harbours in the Complex Interplay between Environment and Society*, p. 42.
2. Wulf Schaefer, *Neue Untersuchungen über die Baugeschichte Nauplias im Mittelalter*, p. 176.
3. Phocion Negris, *Vestiges Antiques Submergés*, p. 352.
4. The bay of Nafplio has been silting up for millennia. In the early Helladic period the sea was a mere 300m from the hill of Tiryns, which is now located almost two kilometres inland. Eberhard Zangger, *Landscape Changes around Tiryns during the Bronze Age*, p. 189.
5. Schaefer, *Neue Untersuchungen*, p. 178 note 17; Gerola, *Fortificazioni*, p. 366; Andrews, *Castles of the Morea*, p. 98.
6. Schaefer's plan of the topography of Nafplio before 1200 (*Neue Untersuchungen*, p. 170) shows the surviving western Byzantine wall and its projected eastern counterpart as well as a harbour area protected by two moles. The eastern mole is on the line described by Negris; the western mole is in the same position as its modern counterpart running from the shore towards the island. Its existence at this time can only be conjecture.
7. Gerola, *Fortificazioni*, pp. 363 and 367.

8. Lurier, *Chronicle of the Morea*, p. 152.
9. Kyllene Harbour Project, www.finninstitute.gr/en/kyllene.
10. Gerola, *Fortificazioni*, p. 355.
11. Diana Wright, *Bartolomeo Minio: Venetian Administration in 15th Century Nauplion*, p. 25 note 11, Gerola, *Fortificazioni*, p. 370.
12. Gerola, *Fortificazioni*, p. 370.
13. Gerola, *Fortificazioni*, p. 389.
14. Diana Wright, *Dispacci from Nauplion*, p. 53.
15. Diana Wright, *Dispacci from Nauplion*, p. 7.
16. Diana Wright, *Dispacci from Nauplion*, p. 165.
17. Gerola, *Fortificazioni*, pp. 372-373.
18. Kevin Andrews, *Castles of the Morea*, p. 100, Gerola, *Fortificazioni*, p. 377, fig. 19 and p. 378, fig. 20.
19. Diana Wright, *Bartolomeo Minio*, p. 59 note 202. Today the porporella is still visible on satellite photographs as a dark ring around the island.
20. Ruth Gertwangen, *Fiscal and Technical Limitations on Venetian Military Engineering in the Stato Da Mar in the Fourteenth and Fifteenth Centuries*, pp. 175-176.
21. Alexander Zäh, *Venezianische Baugeschichte von Nauplia*, p. 153. The aqueduct's route ran along the foot of the north slope of Palamidi. A section is still visible behind the Fire Station. The modern road to Acronauplia is built over the line of the channel but its track can be observed where it emerges from beneath the road, crosses the slope on the eastern side of the Grimani bastion in an arc, and then cuts along the eastern face of the bastion itself. Another channel appears to emerge from the base of the northern face of the bastion. Presumably the aqueduct, first built in the 15C, had to be rerouted when the Grimani bastion was built.
22. Diana Wright, *Bartolomeo Minio*, p. 31.
23. Diana Wright, *Dispacci from Nauplion*, p. 217.
24. Diana Wright, *Dispacci from Nauplion*, p. 279.
25. Francesco Grimani was the Venetian military commander in the Morea from 1699 to 1701 and governor from 1706 to 1708. The portfolio of plans forms the subject matter of Andrews' *Castles of the Morea*.
26. Gerola, *Fortificazioni*, p. 376.
27. Gerola, *Fortificazioni*, pp. 383-385.
28. Alexander Zäh, *Venezianische Baugeschichte von Nauplia*, pp. 145 & 149. Report of Agostino Sagredo, *Δελτίον Ιστορικής και*

Εθνολογικής Εταιρείας της Ελλάδος V, p. 747.
29. Gerola, *Fortificazioni*, p. 382.
30. Kevin Andrews, *Castles of the Morea*, p. 102.
31. This terrace is the *Posto* mentioned by Sagredo in his report to the Venetian Senate of 1714. *Δελτίον* V, p.743. See also Schaefer, *Neue Untersuchungen*, p. 165, Fig. 3.
32. Kevin Andrews, *Castles of the Morea*, p. 100.
33. Kevin Andrews, *Castles of the Morea*, p. 237 and plate XXII.
34. Luca Mola, *Inventors, Patents and the Market for Innovations in Renaissance Italy*, p. 16.
35. Wulf Schaefer, *Neue Untersuchungen*, p. 157 note 2.
36. Kevin Andrews, *Castles of the Morea*, p. 239.
37. Kevin Andrews, *Castles of the Morea*, p. 98.
38. The inverted keyhole form is typical of the earliest gun ports. The vertical slit allowed the weapon to be sighted and the small round opening was sufficient for the small calibre guns of the period. Such gun ports were first introduced in England in the last thirty years of the 14C and in France slightly later. See Kelly DeVries and Robert Douglas Smith, *Medieval Military Technology*, p. 274.
39. Gerola, *Fortificazioni*, p. 355.
40. Diana Wright, *The Second Gate, revisited, and another*, www.surprisedbytime.blogspot.com/2012/06/second-gate-revisited-and-another.html.
41. Alexander Zäh, *Venezianische Baugeschichte von Nauplia*, p. 154.
42. See for example, Wulf Schaefer, *Venezianische Festungsbaukunst in Griechenland*, p. 12, Fig. 6.
43. Kevin Andrews, *Castles of the Morea*, pp. 97-98.

2

The Castle of the Rock (The Bourtzi)

Pasqualigo's sea fort stands on a low reef in the centre of Nafplio bay apparently well preserved. To the Venetians it was the Castello dello Scoglia or the Castello a Mare, the Castle of the Rock or the Castle of the Sea. Today it is usually called the Bourtzi, its name during the Ottoman occupation. Construction began in 1471 under the supervision of Antonio Gambello, Pasqualigo's military engineer, and was probably complete by 1473.[1] The entrance to the port then lay between the fort and the shore and the channel reputedly could be closed by raising a chain between these two points.[2] The fort is a lozenge shaped work approximately 70m by 30m overall. When first built it consisted of a tall central tower with lower gun platforms to the east and west covering the interior of the bay and the seaward approaches. Originally the entire fort seems to have been crenellated with swallow tail merlons above small arched tapering gun ports.[3] The profile of the work viewed from the shore opposite resembles a ship moored in the centre of the bay.

In the decades after its initial construction it became apparent that improvements in military technology had caused the fort to become seriously out of date. Some time after 1525 the central tower was lowered and a new parapet with embrasures for larger artillery was added. The east and west lower batteries were probably altered in the same way.[4] The fort continued in use throughout the two periods of Turkish occupation but was badly damaged in the Greek War of Independence. Although it was subsequently used as the residence of Nafplio's executioners it was a ruin by 1930 when Gerola inspected it. In 1934/5 the architect Wulf Schaefer carried out a survey of Nafplio's surviving monuments and the following year he was responsible for repair work on the Bourtzi.[5] The fort sustained further damage during the Second World War. In the early 1950s it was converted into an hotel based on designs Schaefer had prepared before the war. The hotel closed in the 1970s and all commercial use of the fort ceased in the 1990s. The

The Castle of the Rock

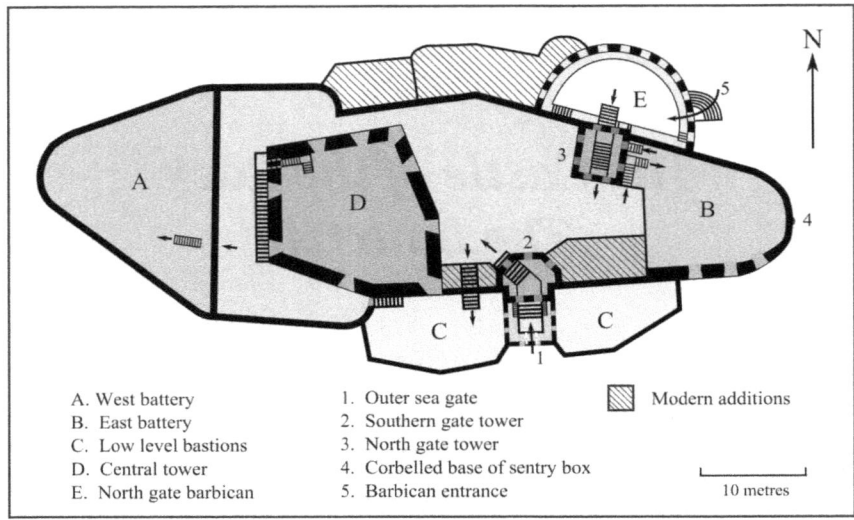

A. West battery
B. East battery
C. Low level bastions
D. Central tower
E. North gate barbican

1. Outer sea gate
2. Southern gate tower
3. North gate tower
4. Corbelled base of sentry box
5. Barbican entrance

▨ Modern additions

10 metres

Plan 7 The Castle of the Rock (The Bourtzi).

interior of the abandoned structure became increasingly derelict but a new programme of restoration is now underway (2017). The fort can usually be visited by boat from the town quay.

The Bourtzi owes its present well-preserved appearance, at least externally, to the restoration work and hotel conversion mentioned above. When Gerola inspected and photographed the derelict structure in 1930 its southern flank and the sea gate were badly damaged. Although the northern side was also in poor condition, sections of its walls survived to a height well above their current level. Both Gerola and Schaefer describe a second line of crenellations built on top of the original parapets of the barbican and the adjacent curtain wall.[6] Schaefer dates these modifications to the period 1480 to 1489. When the fort was repaired the northern walls and the barbican were reduced to their original height, the north gate was rebuilt and the sea gate and its flanking bastions were restored. The hotel conversion involved further modifications. A range of low service buildings was built against the outer face of the north curtain wall, the interior casemates of the main east and west gun platforms were converted into hotel accommodation, existing openings were enlarged and new ones were created to improve access between the various parts of the fort.

Landing at the sea gate must only have been possible in calm conditions and a small boat basin seems to have existed at the eastern end of the reef. Today boats land at a modern stone jetty. The sea gate can

The Castle of the Rock

Fig. 2.1 Bourtzi: The southern face of the fort viewed from the acropolis heights. In the centre is the sea gate.

Fig. 2.2 Bourtzi: The east battery and barbican protecting the north gate. Note the low-level gun port to the right of the gate.

Fig. 2.3 Bourtzi: The interior of the barbican. The entrance to the north gate tower is to the right.

now be reached from the jetty by a concrete walkway but the original access to the fort from this point must have been via the arched door in the north barbican. Steps within the barbican lead to the outer door of the square northern gatehouse tower and also give access to the semi-circular wall walk. Both the barbican and the gatehouse have been restored to their probable original appearance. Their parapets are surmounted by swallow tail merlons and the barbican is equipped with tapering, arched gun ports at ground level. A further flight of steps rises through the interior of the north gate to the raised central court of the fort. To the left of the inner door steps ascend through another arched opening to the gun platform of the eastern battery and from there to the roofs of both gatehouses. The parapet of the eastern gun platform retains three of its open gun embrasures but is clearly much repaired. The base of a sentry box is corbelled out from the extreme eastern tip of the fort. It resembles those found throughout the later Venetian additions to the town's fortifications and may date to the second period of occupation, 1686-1715.

The southern, arched sea gate is set in the wall of a small forebuilding that stands between two low, shallow bastions and leads via a stepped, bent passage through the southern hexagonal gate tower to the central courtyard. On either side of the passage narrow flights of

Fig. 2.4 Bourtzi: The outer doorway of the sea gate and the stairway through the gate tower leading to the central courtyard.

stairs climb to the restored parapet of the forebuilding and from there to the roofs of the low, flanking bastions. A modern door set in the short length of wall connecting the south gate tower to the southeast corner of the central tower provides easier access to the platform of the western, low level bastion. The central tower occupies almost the

The Castle of the Rock

Fig 2.5 Bourtzi: North gate tower, barbican and eastern gun platform.

Fig. 2.6 Bourtzi: The west face of the central tower.

entire western half of the central court. It abuts the southern curtain wall and there is only a narrow corridor between its northern face and the north curtain wall. Its interior is now inaccessible but consisted of two floors above a large cistern fed by water collected on the roof.[7] The structure was modified for heavier artillery after 1525. The original parapet was probably on two levels with a raised wall walk surmounted by the usual swallow tail merlons and tapering vaulted gun ports below at the level of the platform. The arrangement would have resembled the interior of the north barbican. This was replaced by a parapet with splayed open embrasures. The outer faces of the parapets are curved to deflect shot. The roof of the tower is reached by a long external staircase built against the west face of the tower. It rises to a small landing set below the cordon that runs around the exterior walls at the level of the base of the parapet. An arched door between shallow square pilasters opens onto two further interior flights of steps that reach the roof. The truncated pilasters above the doorway indicate where the original parapet was reduced in height.

Access to the western gun battery is via the narrow corridor to the north of the central tower or via modern steps from the western low level bastion. The plain parapet is a modern replacement. No indication of the original survives. Before their conversion into hotel accommodation the interiors of both the east and west batteries consisted of a complex arrangement of casemates equipped with arched gun ports. These spaces are currently inaccessible.

Notes

1. Gerola, *Fortificazioni,* pp. 389-390. Gerola states that after Gambello had begun the project in 1471 it was continued by the engineer Brancaleone who had already built the Venetian fortress at Ravenna known as the Rocca Brancaleone. It is now thought that this attribution is unfounded as no Venetian named Brancaleone can be identified before 1500. See Maurizio Mauro, *La Rocca di Ravenna,* p. 7.
2. Vessels could not pass to the north of the fort as the remainder of the bay was too shallow for safe navigation. Gerola, *Fortificazioni,* p. 389.
3. Wulf Schaefer, *Venezianische Festungsbaukunst in Griechenland. Zum Ausbau der Festung Nauplia,* p. 11.
4. Gerola, *Fortificazioni,* pp. 391-393.
5. Wulf Schaefer, *Neue Untersuchungen,* p. 159.

6. Gerola, *Fortificazioni*, p. 393 and p. 392, fig. 34. Schaefer, *Venezianische Festungsbaukunst*, p. 12. Gerola referred to the barbican as the rondello. He remarked on the evident reworking of the defences over time and observed that the original line of crenellations could still be seen below the raised parapet. He noted a wide variety of loopholes including examples of the inverted keyhole form.
7. Gerola, *Fortificazioni*, p. 393

3

The Acropolis

The development of the fortifications

The first walls of the acropolis, Acronauplia, were built of polygonal masonry around 300BC. They began at the southwest tip of the peninsula and ran north and east along the crest of the slopes overlooking the harbour. To the south the precipitous cliffs were regarded as sufficient defence. The east wall was built at the edge of a natural terrace leaving the eastern tail of the acropolis hill unenclosed. Here stood the main gate of the fortress (Plan 3, 6). There may also have been western and northern gates to provide access to the port. (see below). When new Byzantine walls arose on the hill they followed the same line and were built directly on top of the surviving courses of the ancient wall. The east wall was reinforced with three semicircular towers. The southern pair of towers flanked the main gate. These two towers were subsequently increased in height and thickness transforming them from a round form to a pointed or pentagonal plan. Schaefer dated the round towers to the second half of the 3C around the time of Claudius II and the second phase of building to the late 4C.[1] As before the southern end of the eastern defences ended abruptly at the cliff edge.

The Frankish siege of Nafplio in 1212 ended with a negotiated surrender. The treaty made provision for the acropolis to be divided into two fortified areas split between the original inhabitants and the invaders. The two areas created were thereafter to become known as the Castle of the Franks and the Castle of the Greeks.[2] The Franks built, or possibly re-built, a crosswall from the north curtain to the southern cliff edge creating a separate, eastern enclosure for themselves that occupied approximately one quarter of the total area of the acropolis. In plan this wall formed an obtuse angle. At the apex the Franks built a tall tower with walls over two metres thick that projected west, flanking the wall and commanding the western enclosure of the Greeks.[3] A gate in the crosswall to the south of the tower gave access to the Greek

The Acropolis

Fig. 3.1 Acronauplia: The northwest walls. More than six courses of the 3C BC walls survive beneath the mediaeval work.

Fig. 3.2 Acronauplia: The inner east gate after recent conservation.

town. In effect, the Franks created a typical western mediaeval arrangement of castle (the Frankish enclosure) and attached walled town (the Castle of the Greeks) with the castle fortified against both external threats and from the Greek town to the west.

The Byzantine main gate in the east wall of the circuit continued to be the entrance to the Frankish enclosure. The gate was remodelled by the Franks and around 1300 the interior was decorated with a remarkable series of frescoes.[4] It is usually suggested that this gate remained the single entrance to the acropolis enclosures and that the Castle of the Greeks could only be accessed by traversing the Frankish enclosure. However this would have allowed free access to the Franks' carefully fortified enclave, a situation that could only be avoided if another external gate to the Castle of the Greeks existed. One candidate for such a separate entrance may have stood on the site of a possible earlier Byzantine north gate. The Camocio map of Nafplio from 1571 shows a gate in the north wall where it jogs to the south for some twenty metres.[5] If this map is an accurate representation, and such plans were heavily stylised, then the gate must have existed when the Venetians abandoned Nafplio in 1540 and possibly considerably earlier. A walled up gate exists at this point today (Plan 8, 4), but it dates only from the second Venetian occupation.[6] Nevertheless this is the most likely location for a gate giving separate access to the Castle of the Greeks. It would also have provided a much more direct route from the port to the upper town. The survival of the Frankish frescoes in the east main gate seems to provide indirect evidence that it was never used as the main thoroughfare to the upper town. The frescoes date from the period 1291 to 1311 and the gate continued in use until 1463 when it was blocked up by the Venetians.[7] The paintings were first discovered in 1957. They were in remarkably good condition when first revealed and covered the entire interior surface of the gate's inner chamber. Their survival over the period of one hundred and fifty years when the gate was open does not seem possible if it had been subject to continuous heavy traffic.

When the Venetians first arrived in Nafplio they did little more than patch up the acropolis walls and the original mediaeval character of the fortifications remained unchanged. When war broke out in 1463 and Argos fell to the Turks, the inherent weakness of these relatively thin, vertical, mediaeval walls became apparent. The east gate was particularly vulnerable as it was unshielded from direct bombardment. The Venetian response was to brick up the gate and fill the interior chambers with earth. Schaefer implies that this was done as soon as war with the Turks broke out, but it may have happened only

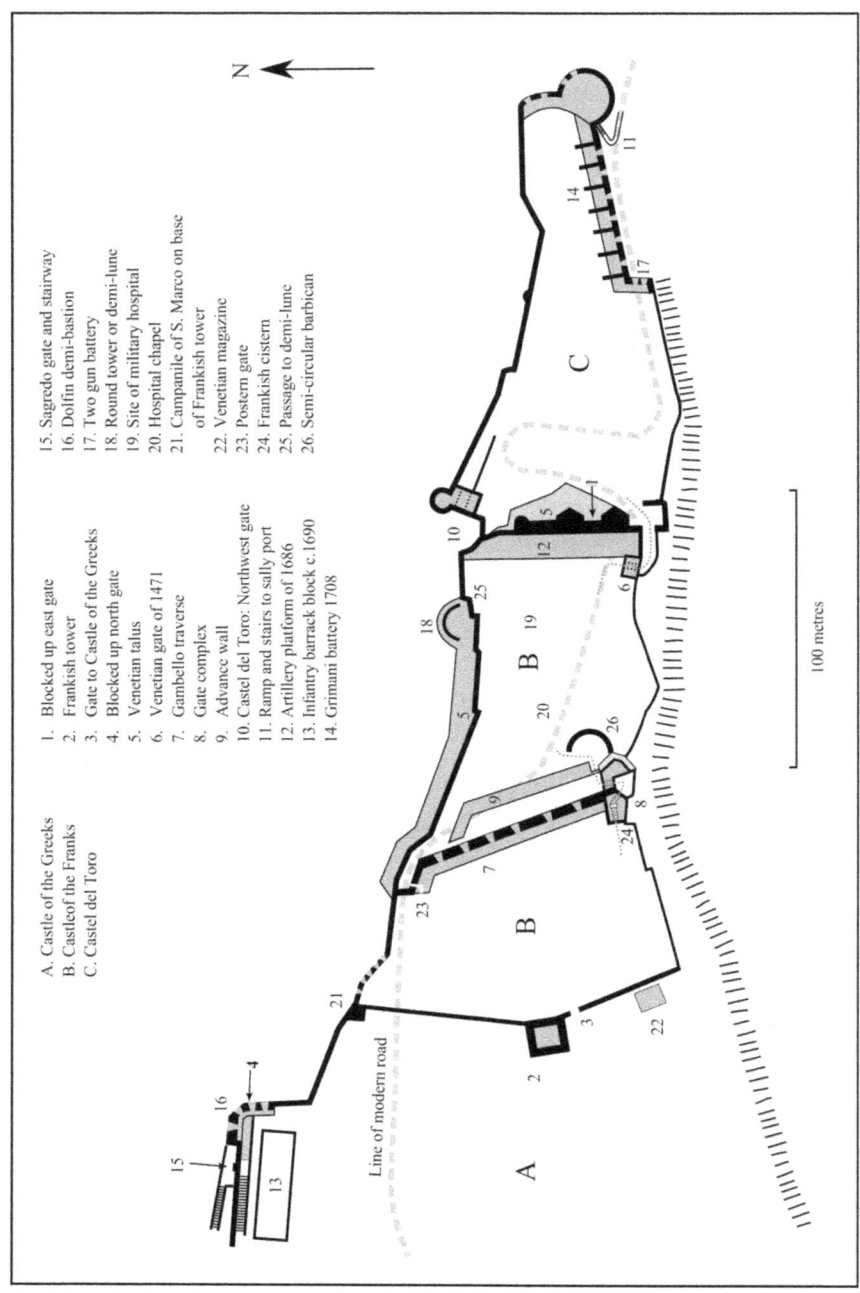

Plan 8 The eastern acropolis fortifications until the early 20C.

The Acropolis

when Pasqualigo began his comprehensive reform of the fortifications in 1470.[8] On the acropolis this programme of reconstruction had three main elements. The first involved strengthening the walls already in existence. This was achieved by building a massive talus against the exterior of the east and north walls of the Castle of the Franks. It completely enveloped the eastern towers and gate and was designed to deflect the impact of cannon shot. The now buried east gate was replaced by a new entrance on a protected alignment facing south (Plan 8, 6) approached via a terrace built on the cliff edge at the southern tip of the east wall.[9]

The second element of the programme to be constructed was a new defensive line 100m to the west of the east wall. Now known as the Gambello traverse, after Pasqualigo's military engineer, this rampart roughly bisects the original enclosure of the Franks and was provided with its own gate complex at the southern end. Its battered wall supported a broad artillery platform facing east. A lower, advance wall a few metres to the east was designed to protect the base of the main

Fig. 3.3 Acronauplia: The Gambello traverse and entrance complex with their restored parapets. In the foreground the curved outwork or barbican protecting the entrance arch in the surviving section of the advance wall.

The Acropolis

Fig. 3.4 Acronauplia: Southern sally port in the round tower of Castel del Toro. Right is the south face of the Grimani bastion.

wall from bombardment. The face of this shield wall sloped at forty-five degrees and was intended to deflect shot. A wall may also have been built for the first time on the southern side of the enclosure between the two new gates.

The third and largest element of Pasqualigo's work was the creation of new walls enclosing the unprotected eastern tail of the acropolis hill. Named Castel del Toro after the great, heavily battered, round tower at its eastern tip, this new enclosure dominated the approach from the east and flanked the land gate of the town. A gate at the northwest corner of the new enceinte was constructed to give access down the lower town (Plan 8, 10). A sally port in the southwest flank of the round tower (Plan 8, 11) gave access via steps and a ramp to the southern beach below.[10]

However this ambitious undertaking was not fully completed during the years of Pasqualigo's governorship. Much of the work seems to have been carried out in great haste. Minio reported in 1479 that he was having to rebuild "the scarp which protects the Castle of the Franks at the curtain wall by the gate where the scarp has collapsed".[11] The Gambello traverse was only completed during the tenure of Zaccaria Barbaro, governor after Pasqualigo.[12] Castel del Toro must have been completed by 1479 when Minio arrived. He refers to the fortification by name in January 1482.[13] However the rampart and embrasures of the round tower itself may have been rebuilt around 1500 when it was equipped with vaulted gun embrasures within the thickness of the parapet. The chambers taper to arched openings in the outer face. They survive in reasonable condition today and bear comparison to the work at Methoni known as the Bembo bastion dating to 1494.[14] Based on the presence of two shields below a lion of St. Mark above the entrance to the sally port, Gerola attempted to date the entire work to around 1500, during the period when Nafplio was governed by two magistrates (1493-1516). However in a note he concedes that other emblems with two shields can be found elsewhere on the walls dating from Pasqualigo's time and their presence may simply signify work carried out by two consecutive magistrates.[15]

After the Venetians returned to Nafplio in 1686 the entire acropolis became a military area. An artillery platform was created against the east wall of the Castle of the Franks soon after 1686 by building a retaining wall fifteen metres to the west of the old wall and filling the intervening space with earth.[16] An earthwork redoubt facing east was built in the centre of the old enclosure of the Castle of the Greeks at about the same time. This subsequently shielded cavalry stables built between 1701 and 1706 (Plan 5, 21). To the north of the redoubt a large infantry barrack block was erected in the 1690s. An even larger cavalry barracks to the west followed in 1705-08. The fortifications were improved further with the re-modelling of the southeast face of Castel del Toro by Francesco Grimani in 1708 to create a new gun battery with six deep embrasures covering the foreshore below (Plan 8, 14).[17]

The most elaborate addition however was the creation in 1713 of a new monumental gate in the north wall of the Castle of the Greeks near to the infantry barracks, with a stairway leading down the cliff directly to the centre of the lower town. A tall, narrow tower, or demi-bastion, had been built here earlier at the corner where the north curtain makes a twenty metre jog to the south. Erected during the governorship of Daniele Dolfin between 1701 and 1704, this structure incorporated an arched gate in its east face. Set between two pilasters, the gate led into a corridor running against the inner face of the wall with steps rising to the level of the barracks above.[18] This gate may represent the last rebuilding of a much earlier entrance and it must have been walled up when Agostino Sagredo completed the new monumental gate a few metres to the west of the Dolfin demi-bastion. The approach to the new gate involved the construction of a stairway of two zig-zag flights leading to a landing in the angle formed by the north wall and the west flank of the Dolfin tower. The upper flight is

The Acropolis

Fig. 3.5 Acronauplia: The Dolfin demi-bastion. The arch of the walled-up gate can be seen in its east flank.

Fig 3.6 Acronauplia: The Sagredo gate at the head of the stairs from the lower town, now dominated by the Xenia Palace hotel.

carried on arches built over the rocks of the cliff (Fig. 3.6). Two ornamental pillars with pyramidal capping stones stand at the head of the stairs. The gate itself is set in a round arch within an avant-corps of rough masonry with a cornice and pediment above. The gate opening leads via an arched chamber into the stepped corridor mentioned above. Sagredo also remodelled the Dolfin demi-bastion adding a battery of four artillery embrasures to the parapet.[19]

The fortifications of the acropolis today

The north and east profiles of Castel del Toro when seen from below appear to retain much of their original appearance although the interior is dominated by the shell of the derelict Xenia hotel. The best preserved elements are the round tower and the adjacent section of the north wall that curves to meet it. The parapet of the tower is equipped with two open and four vaulted embrasures. The adjacent curve of the north wall is at a slightly lower level and has two open embrasures. From below this configuration gives the impression of a double round tower (Fig. 1.10). However the south front of Castel del Toro has been almost completely destroyed by modern construction. Until 1935 the southern walls stood on the edge of the cliff that rose from the beach below. The rock-cut ditch separating the Grimani bastion from the Palamidi slopes made a right-angle turn west where it opened onto the wide rocky foreshore. A ramp led from the beach to the foot of the steps up to the southern sally port in the round tower. To the west of the tower the south wall supported the long Grimani battery of 1708. At the western end of the line of six embrasures the wall jogged south for fifteen metres. Here the parapet was equipped with two gun embrasures facing east to flank the ditch. From this point a relatively thin wall connected the battery to the east wall of the Castle of the Franks.[20]

In 1935 Schaefer was engaged to build the first access road to the acropolis from the lower town. The road followed the line of the ditch around the Grimani bastion then climbed the slope beneath the south wall of Castel del Toro partially cut into the cliff and partially built out on a retaining wall. Its line ran straight through the east facing battery which was totally demolished. A long serpentine curve led into the interior of the enclosure and through a breach in the east wall of the Castle of the Franks (see below). Every structure within the walls of Toro, including a Turkish house, was demolished at this time.[21] When the Xenia hotel was established in 1961 the little that was left within the enclosure was completely swept away. The interior was levelled

The Acropolis

Fig. 3.7 Acronauplia c. 1930. The Grimani battery of 1708 within Castel del Toro is still intact. In the foreground is part of the southern stepped caponier. Source: *Gerola*, Fortificazioni, Fig. 10.

Fig. 3.8 The acropolis fortifications in 2014 taken from approximately the same position.

The Acropolis

Fig. 3.9 Acronauplia: The gun platform of the round tower of Castel del Toro. The steps visible in the old hotel garden lead to the entrances of the vaulted passageways within the tower.

and the line of the original south wall of the Grimani battery was extended west to support a level platform for the hotel building. At the same time the access road was widened and re-aligned. The platform of the round tower was incorporated into the hotel gardens that occupied the eastern end of the enclosure. However the landscaping preserved access to the sunken entrance to the vaulted passages within the body of tower (Plan 6,7). The low, stepped northern passage, cut two centuries after Castel del Toro was first built, tunnels through the tower to the door above the Grimani bastion discussed above. A pointed arch frames the entrance to the sloping southern passage which descends to the sally port halfway up the outer face of the tower. A modern flight of steps now leads down to the access road built over the original approach ramp (Fig. 3.4).

The original route to Castel del Toro from the lower town follows the stepped lane that climbs past the Catholic church (Plan 2,8) before turning east to Pasqualigo's gate. This rectangular gatehouse stands in the northwest angle of Castel del Toro where the long, battered, northern wall makes a right angle turn south to meet the northeast angle of the Castle of the Franks. A round tower projects from the corner of the gatehouse. The flat roofs of the gatehouse and tower form one

The Acropolis

Fig. 3.10 Acronauplia: Gate to Castel del Toro built by Pasqualigo.

platform with a continuous crenellated parapet. The lane passes through an outer arched gate into a central chamber and then through an inner gate set in a barrel vaulted passage. The inner chamber is equipped with a murder hole in the vault and a stepped passage opening off the south wall that once gave access to the roof. A torus moulding runs around the tower, across the face of the gate at the level of the arch, emphasising the unity of the architecture. Above the outer gate a winged lion and a shield are set in the face of the wall. This approach to the acropolis still preserves much of the fortifications' original appearance. The parapet of the gate has no doubt been repaired many times over the centuries and until recently it was formed of close-spaced rectangular merlons pierced by tapering loopholes. The swallow tail form of merlon has now been restored and the result probably resembles the original. Overlooking the road to the gate the Venetians incorporated a semi-circular tower, or demi-lune, into the slope of the massive talus they built against the north wall of the Castle of the Franks (Plan 8, 18). Again its parapet is of notched merlons pierced by loopholes but in this case the isolated position of the tower suggests

The Acropolis

they may be original. Access to the platform of the demi-lune from within the Castle of the Franks is via a stepped dog-leg passage leading beneath the original north wall to a doorway emerging from an angle of the talus (Plan 8, 25). This access route has recently been restored.

The lane continues uphill beyond the gate and emerges onto the curve of the modern access road directly in front of the derelict hotel. Although the road and hotel have obliterated everything within the enclosure of Castel del Toro, the massive east curtain of the Castle of the Franks survives. The partial collapse of the Venetian talus around the northern tower has been consolidated recently but the round profile of the earliest tower can still be seen within the enveloping masonry. Similarly the top of the middle pentagonal tower emerges from the peak of the talus slope. The outer entrance to the original east gate remains hidden behind the talus. The greater part of the southern tower was demolished in 1928 to create a new route into the upper enclosures.[22] This destruction exposed elements of the tower's internal structure. In creating the breach the end of the wall retaining the artillery platform of 1686 was removed, exposing the earth infill. In 1935, when Schaefer was building the first access road, he removed more of this earth infill and discovered the inner face of the east gate. A new wall was subsequently built to retain the exposed end of the

Fig. 3.11 Castle of the Franks: The Venetian talus built around the towers of the east wall.

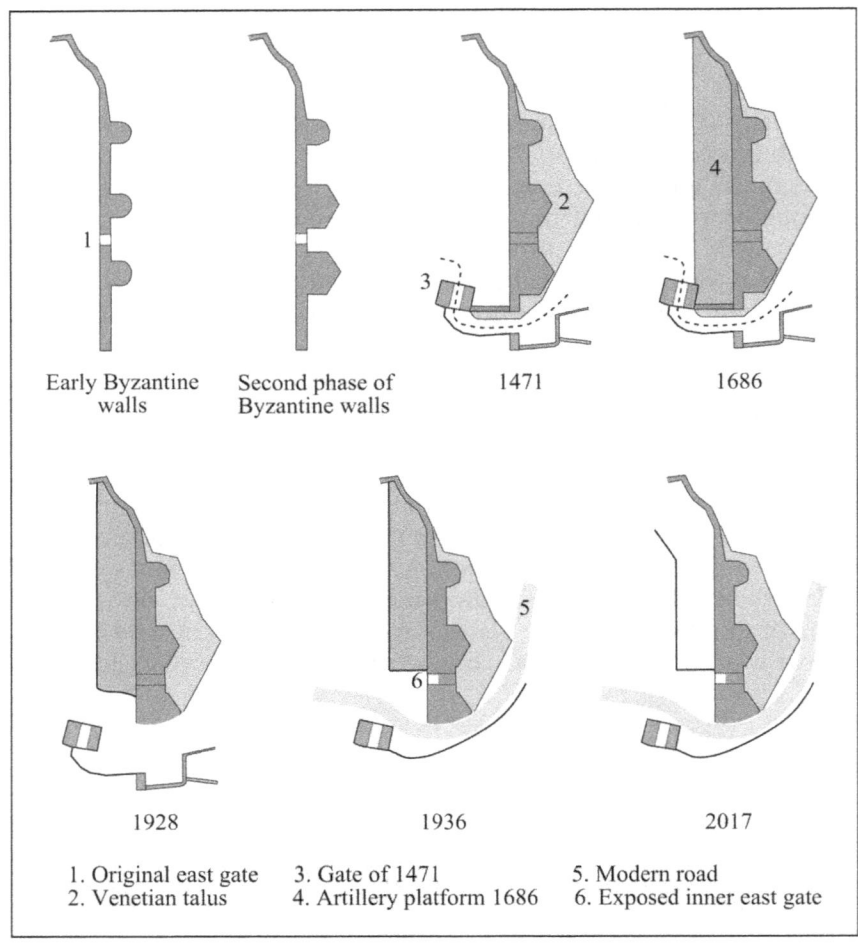

Plan 9 The development of the east front of the Castle of the Franks. Derived from *Schaefer*, Das Stadttor, Fig. 5.

earth terrace and protect the face of the newly revealed gate. Recently the remaining elements of the Venetian platform have been removed. This has revealed the inner face of the original Byzantine wall and allowed access to the interior of the middle tower. The inner chamber of the east gate has been conserved and the frescoes are visible inside a protective barrier. The interior approach to the gate has been cleared down to its original level (Fig. 3.2).

The new gatehouse facing south that the Venetians built around 1471 to replace the blocked up original is now isolated on the edge of the cliff. Although the inner face is half obscured by the level of the modern road the entrance passage is still accessible. Its sloping pavement is crossed by ridges of raised cobbles that would have assisted horses and pack animals making the ascent. The outer face of the gatehouse now stands above a precipice. The terrace that supported the approach has either been demolished or has fallen down the cliff.[23]

Beyond the east wall the road passes the site of the 19C military hospital. This was demolished around 1970 but the hospital chapel, the church of St. Anargyroi, still stands by the roadside. Ahead is the massive wall of the Gambello traverse, its southern gate complex masked by a curved outwork. The outline of this heavily battered wall with its long rank of notched merlons is striking, but the parapet is entirely modern. Kevin Andrews writing in about 1950, stated that the wall formed a revetment to the higher ground to the west and supported six gun embrasures, although by that date they were little more than heaps of earth. The ruined embrasures can be seen in old photographs and are clearly shown on the Grimani plans.[24] The parapet seen today was built in 1976 by the Greek construction engineer Petidis as part of a scheme to consolidate the crumbling walls. The reconstruction appears to be based on Schaefer's drawing of 1936 and

Fig. 3.12 Castle of the Franks: the Venetian gate of 1471.

The Acropolis

Fig. 3.13 Gambello traverse: Outer gate of the entrance complex with its restored merlons. Centre left is the stub of the demolished advance wall.

both the swallow tail merlons and the small arched embrasures of his sketch are accurately reproduced.[25] Schaefer's view of the original form of the parapet was based on his work on the Bourtzi. When first constructed this was crenellated throughout with notched merlons above small arched tapering gun ports. As the Gambello traverse dates to the same period it may have followed the same pattern. Presumably, just as the Bourtzi was subsequently updated for heavier artillery, then so too was the traverse. The advance shield wall built in front of the traverse has been almost completely demolished but a ten metre long section survives at the southern end where it abuts the face of the irregular tower, or bastion, protecting the outer gate. This section contains the arched entrance that provided the original route to the gate (Fig. 3.3). The opening in the advance wall is the only element of the gate complex that was vulnerable to direct fire from the east and it was therefore protected by a semi-circular rampart, or barbican. Kevin Andrews thought the plain, uncrenellated parapet signified that the entire structure was Turkish, but the work also resembles the semi-circular barbican of the Bourtzi with its thin loopholes above two low arched gun ports. It is probably Venetian of the same period as the traverse but perhaps with a later Turkish parapet.[26]

Fig. 3.14 Gambello traverse: Interior of the entrance courtyard. The inner gatehouse is to the left. The shield below the relief of a Venetian lion originally held the three bands of the Pasqualigo crest.

The arch of the outer gate is aligned at right-angles to the plane of the traverse and leads south beneath a vaulted wall-walk into a small pentagonal courtyard. The wall-walk connects a door in the east face of the inner gate tower with the terreplein of the irregular bastion that forms the east side of the court. A low, thin wall built over the vertical cliff encloses the south side, while to the west stands the five sided inner gatehouse tower built across the southern end of the traverse. The inner gate leads into a bent, sloping corridor of two arched passages separated by a section open to the sky. The gatehouse roof platform and parapet are raised about a metre above the level of the traverse. Steps down from the platform reach the door giving access to the eastern bastion (visible in Fig. 3.3). When Andrews photographed the gate complex only a solitary pair of notched merlons survived above the outer gate.[27] The parapets have now been thoroughly restored in the same manner as the traverse, presumably at the same time. A large cistern, which Schaefer believed to be Frankish, can be seen on the left where the entrance passage emerges from the gatehouse (Plan 8, 24). Most of the area immediately to the west of the traverse is now given over to large, concrete, twentieth century cisterns built partially on top of an earlier Venetian example. A massive, modern water pipe runs through the gate passages to connect to these cisterns. Its installation has destroyed the gate thresholds and the pavement of the passageways. At its northern end the Gambello traverse made a dog-leg turn before meeting the north curtain of the Castle of the Franks. This deviation created a narrow, blind passageway that concealed a postern gate (Plan 8, 23). The modern road has been driven through this passage and a short section of the traverse has been demolished where it joined the curtain. The opening of the postern gate in the outer wall has been all but buried by the built up surface of the modern road. Only the top of the arch is now visible. However on the inner face of the traverse the archway and stepped passage that leads down to the gate survive intact.

Fifty metres to the west of the traverse are the fragmentary remains of the original west wall of the Castle of the Franks. It exists now as a few courses of rubble to the south of the great square tower which itself is now only a stump. Just enough of the northern section of the wall survives to indicate the change of angle. Recent consolidation work has taken place. The campanile of the demolished church of San Marco stands on the base of another Frankish tower where the crosswall joined the north curtain.[28] Towards the southern end of the wall

Fig. 3.15 Castle of the Franks: The stub of the Frankish tower. To the right is the pyramid roof of the Venetian powder magazine.

on its western side stands a square, pyramid-roofed magazine built in 1713. This is the only surviving Venetian military building on the acropolis following the demolition of the barrack blocks and cavalry stables described above.[29]

Fig. 3.16 Acronauplia: The interior stairway of the Sagredo gate.

West of the campanile the northern side of the acropolis is dominated by modern hotel installations on the site of the demolished Venetian barracks. The interior of the Sagredo gate (Figs. 3.6 and 3.16) is now concealed by these buildings and can only be inspected from within the hotel grounds as the door between the gate chamber and the external stairway is permanently closed. The square entrance chamber within the gate leads immediately to a long monumental staircase rising east to west along the inner face of the north wall. The lower half of the stairway is vaulted. The east wall of the gate chamber reveals no trace of an earlier corridor leading to the walled up gateway in the east face of the Dolfin demi-bastion. Presumably this was obliterated when the bastion was re-modelled. The external stairway from the lower town and the façade of the Sagredo gate survive as described above but are in increasingly poor condition. The east flank of the Dolfin demi-bastion and the earlier walled up gate can most easily be seen from the adjacent north curtain wall. The parapet of the bastion has been largely destroyed but one of its gun embrasures survives as does the base of a sentry box corbelled out from the northeast corner.

At the western end of the peninsula there are two further elements of the fortifications dating from the second Venetian occupation. The

Fig. 3.17 Acronauplia: The western gun battery.

Fig. 3.18 Acronauplia: The gate created by Morosini viewed from the parapet above. The crude arch is visible within the rubble infill.

first is the gate created by Morosini in 1686 to give access to the shore below via precipitous steps down the cliff (Plan 5, 18). The gate is located where a tall section of the curtain wall blocked off the head of a gulley. The opening was inserted at the base of the wall either by almost completely removing the early polygonal walling or by utilising an existing breach. The wall was then rebuilt to its original height in roughly coursed rubble masonry with tile in-filling. The arched outer face of the gate is crudely constructed and the opening was later roughly walled up. Steps must have existed on the inner side but the area has now been levelled with modern debris. It has been suggested that this is the site of a Byzantine west gate but the complete rebuilding of the wall above the gate has left no evidence of earlier masonry styles.[30] At the extreme southwestern tip of the peninsula, guarded by a scrub of dense prickly pear, is the final element of the defences, a battery of three gun positions built on the cliff edge. Presumably designed to command the sea approaches, it consists of three embrasures, two arched and one open, set in a plain parapet.

Fig. 3.19 Acronauplia: One of the three WWII gun emplacements showing the central gun pivot and the concrete traversing ring.

Fig. 3.20 Acronauplia: The concrete roofed WWII observation post.

The Acropolis

The acropolis saw one final period of military use during the Second World War when a three gun battery facing south was constructed on the highest point of the acropolis ridge by the occupying forces. The three identical emplacements each have a central pivot point surrounded by a six metre diameter concrete traversing ring, an underground bunker to the rear, possibly the magazine, with a concrete slit trench opposite, presumably for the protection of the gunners. An observation post, roughly constructed of rubble masonry with a crude but thick concrete roof, was located near the cliff edge between the western and centre emplacements.

Notes

1. Wulf Schaefer, *Neue Untersuchungen*, p. 178, *Das Stadttor von Akronauplia*, p. 24. Schaefer refers to the reformed towers as "half a regular hexagon in plan".
2. Harold Lurier, *Crusaders as Conquerors: the Chronicle of the Morea*, p. 155. "Now Nauplion happens to be a castle on two crags; therefore, they negotiated that the first be surrendered and the other, the weaker one, the Romans would retain". This much quoted passage has been used to argue that the division was between two existing enclosures. However there is no clear evidence that the Byzantine circuit was ever divided by a cross-wall and it may be that the passage simply reflected the topography of the acropolis where the eastern defences with the main gate and flanking towers were thought to be the strongest part of the circuit.
3. Schaefer, *Neue Untersuchungen*, p. 191. The tower survived until the 19C. When Schaefer saw and measured the ruin in 1934 it was reduced to a height of five metres. He compares its appearance to that of the Frankish keep at Acrocorinth.
4. The gate had been hidden until 1935 when Schaefer removed the earth infill of the Venetian artillery platform that concealed it. He was not able to begin excavation until 1956 when he exposed the gate's chambers still filled with soil. The frescoes were revealed by subsequent campaigns in 1957 and 1958 but the findings were only ever partially published. Schaefer, *Neue Untersuchungen*, p. 175. For a complete examination of the frescoes using many of Schaefer's original photographs see Monika Hirschbichler, *The Crusader Paintings in the Frankish Gate At Nauplia, Greece*.

5. www.Nauplion.net/Camoccio map.html
6. This gate was first discussed by Diana Wright. Previously it seems to have gone unnoticed. See Diana Wright, *The Second Gate*, www.surprisedbytime.blogspot.com/2010/04/second-gate.html However it is shown clearly on Schaefer's overall plan of Nafplio. Schaefer, *Neue Untersuchungen*, p. 161, Fig. 1.
7. Monika Hirschbichler, *Crusader Paintings*, p. 21.
8. Schaefer, *Neue Untersuchungen*, p. 167. If the gate was blocked up soon after 1463 this would be a further indication that a second northern gate must have existed at this time as the new gate in the east wall was built no earlier than 1471.
9. Wulf Schaefer, *Das Stadttor von Akronauplia*, p. 20. The artillery platform behind the east wall (Plan 8, 12) may have been constructed at this time but Schaefer dates it to 1686.
10. G. Gerola, *Fortificazioni*, pp. 363-362; K. Andrews, *Castles of the Morea*, pp. 95-97.
11. Diana Wright, *Dispacci from Nauplion*, p. 9.
12. A plaque with Barbaro's crest, his initials and the date 1473 can be seen beneath the parapet in the centre of the traverse. Gerola found this plaque in 1930 built into the pillars of a nearby modern bell tower. It was probably replaced in 1976. G. Gerola, *Fortificazioni*, p. 360.
13. Diana Wright, *Dispacci from Nauplion*, p. 211.
14. Pepper, *Fortress and Fleet*, p. 36.
15. Gerola, *Fortificazioni*, pp. 365-366 and note 3.
16. Wulf Schaefer, *Das Stadttor von Akronauplia*, pp. 20-23. In recent years this earth infill has been removed.
17. Zäh, *Venezianische Baugeschichte von Nauplia*, pp. 152 and 146.
18. Gerola, *Fortificazioni*, p. 357; Kevin Andrews, *Castles of the Morea*, p. 100; Diana Wright, *www.surprisedbytime.blogspot.com /2010/03/last-hurrah-at-nauplion.html*.
19. Gerola, *Fortificazioni*, p. 359; Kevin Andrews, *Castles of the Morea*, p. 103; Alexander Zäh, *Venezianische Baugeschichte von Nauplia*, pp. 153-154.
20. Schaefer, *Neue Untersuchungen*, p. 161, Fig. 1; Gerola, *Fortificazioni*, p. 362, Fig. 10.
21. Andrews, *Castles of the Morea*, p. 92, Fig. 98; Schaefer, *Neue Untersuchungen*, p. 160.
22. Schaefer, *Das Stadttor*, p. 21, Fig. 5.
23. Ibid. Schaefer's plan of 1936 marks a section of the approach as already fallen away.

24. Kevin Andrews, *Castles of the Morea*, p. 92, Fig. 98; p. 94, Fig. 100; p. 95. Plate XXI shows the fortifications as recorded by the Venetians in 1686. The six embrasures of the Gambello traverse are clearly marked.
25. Wulf Schaefer, *Venezianische Festungsbaukunst in Griechenland*, p. 11 and p. 10, Fig. 4. Schaefer explains that Petidis added the crenellations "of his own accord" but seems too modest to link their appearance to his own drawings from 1936.
26. Andrews, *Castles of the Morea*, p. 100.
27. Andrews, *Castles of the Morea*, p. 95.
28. Alexander Zäh, *Venezianische Baugeschichte*, p. 164, Ref. 8.
29. Alexander Zäh, *Venezianische Baugeschichte*, p. 147.
30. Gerola, *Fortificazioni*, p. 357.

4

The Palamidi Fortifications

The Venetians were never in any doubt about the strategic importance of the Palamidi heights. In 1686 Morosini himself had bombarded the Turks in the town below from this position and control of the mountain top was clearly essential for Nafplio's future security. Unfortunately the scale of the fortifications required to secure the whole ridge meant that plans to carry out the work were repeatedly deferred as too expensive. A detailed design for a network of artillery bastions or forts covering the hill was drawn up for Francesco Grimani by the military engineer Giaxich in 1707 but the only work actually carried out was the erection of the rampart and caponier built on the lower slopes opposite the Grimani bastion[1] (see p.20 above). Construction based on Giaxich's designs finally began in 1711 on the initiative of Agostino Sagredo. Progress was rapid and the works were substantially complete by the end of 1714.[2] Despite this monumental effort the entire complex of forts fell to the invading Ottoman forces in July 1715 after a brief bombardment.[3] The Turks later completed the few unfinished sections of the defences following the original Venetian plans. They also added yet another outwork which extended the fortifications a further 100M southwards along the ridge. After the War of Independence sections of the fortress were converted into prisons, initially Forts Miltiades and Andreas, and later the Venetian barrack blocks within Fort Themistocles. The prisons closed in 1923 and the barrack blocks were demolished in the 1950s.[4]

Overview of the fortifications

By the early 18C the bastioned trace had become the standard form for any major works of fortification. With polygonal bastions connected by broad curtain walls the system provided near perfect flanking protection. The bastions and walls were typically massive earthworks

Palamidi Fortifications

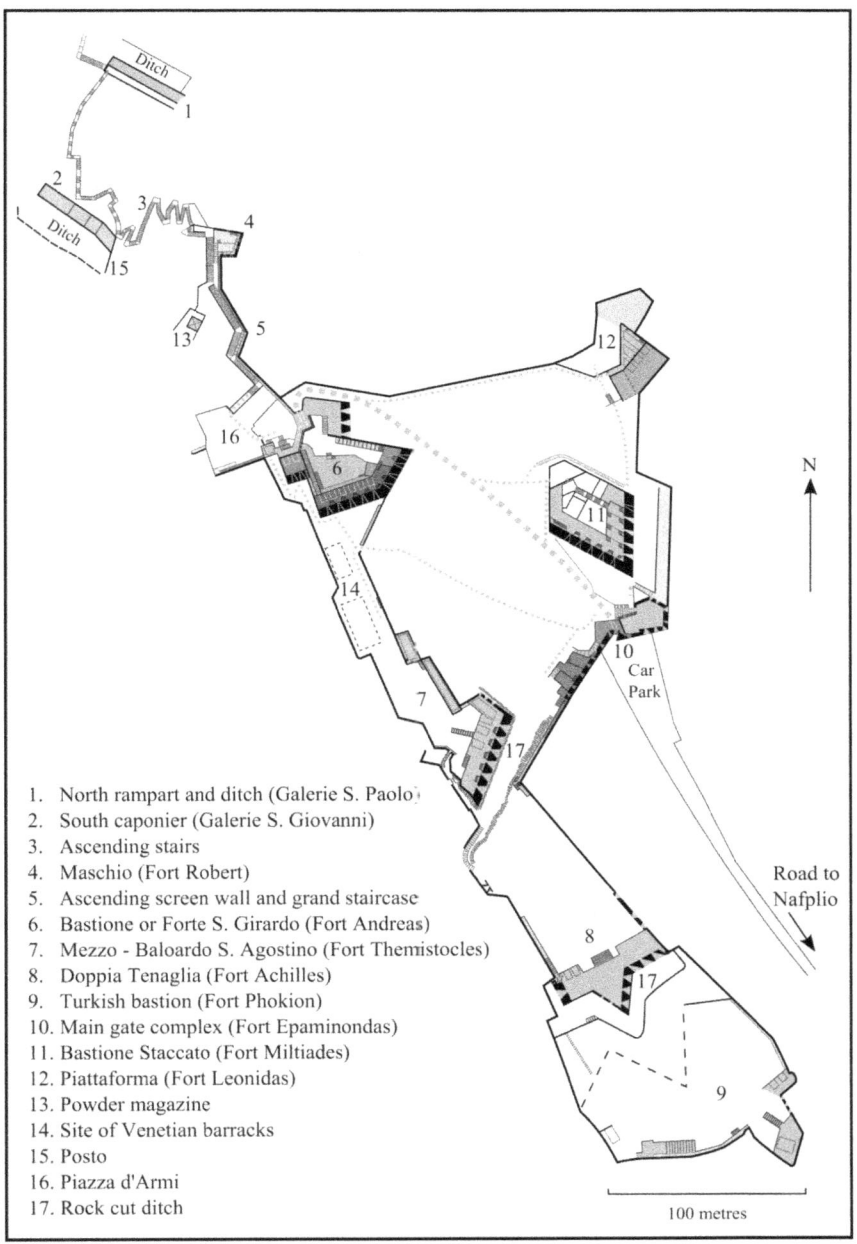

1. North rampart and ditch (Galerie S. Paolo)
2. South caponier (Galerie S. Giovanni)
3. Ascending stairs
4. Maschio (Fort Robert)
5. Ascending screen wall and grand staircase
6. Bastione or Forte S. Girardo (Fort Andreas)
7. Mezzo - Baloardo S. Agostino (Fort Themistocles)
8. Doppia Tenaglia (Fort Achilles)
9. Turkish bastion (Fort Phokion)
10. Main gate complex (Fort Epaminondas)
11. Bastione Staccato (Fort Miltiades)
12. Piattaforma (Fort Leonidas)
13. Powder magazine
14. Site of Venetian barracks
15. Posto
16. Piazza d'Armi
17. Rock cut ditch

Plan 10 Overview of the Palamidi fortification complex.
Derived from *Schaefer*, Neue Untersuchungen, Fig. 3.

with masonry revetments protected by a wide ditch, usually dry, with a sloping glacis beyond. Outworks were employed to keep attacking artillery further from the main line of the fortifications and became increasingly elaborate as the science of fortification developed.

While the land front of the lower town constructed between 1702 and 1711 largely conformed to this schema, the topography and geology of the Palamidi hill and the absence of virtually any level area precluded a design involving a symmetrical bastioned layout. In addition the rocky terrain made the construction of an extensive system of ditches virtually impossible. The solution adopted by Giaxich was to abandon the concept of a continuous trace and utilise instead a network of individual artillery redoubts located to command each of the vulnerable areas of the mountain, both the main north-south ridge and the gentler slopes to the east and northeast. The inner components of the fortifications would command and protect those beyond to produce a system of defence in depth.

The centrepiece of the system is Bastione S. Girardo (Fort Andreas). The main body of this work is an irregular pentagon, built on a slope at the northwestern extremity of the ridge overlooking the town below. Although the highest point of the ridge is almost 200m further south, the towering proportions of this bastion allows its main battery to command the entire length of the Mezzo-baloardo S. Agostino (Fort Themistokles) to the south. S. Agostino functions as a major outwork to S. Girardo. Its walls enclose the long slope of the ridge and terminate at a large gun platform commanding the southern approaches and the interior of the original final outwork, the Doppia Tenaglia, the double pincer, now known as Fort Achilles. This hornwork, separated from Agostino by a rock-cut ditch, extends the line of fortifications a further 100m to the south and terminates in another large gun platform, in this case with a triangular beak at its centre. A further rock cut ditch separated it from the remainder of the ridge. However the relatively level ground to the south was still regarded as a weakness in the defences. The Venetians had started to build a type of ravelin, or bonnet, beyond the ditch,[5] but it was the Turks after 1715 who added the outwork now known as Fort Phokion. This large irregular structure is again designed to support gun batteries at its southern end to cover the country beyond. Each of these successive outworks is open at the rear so that if overrun by an enemy it provided no protection from fire from the inner works.

To the west of this long line of fortifications the ground falls steeply down to the sea and needed no further defences. However the northern and eastern flanks of the mountain slope more gently and further fortifications were required to deny these approaches to an attacking force. The Bastione Staccato (Fort Miltiades) is a freestanding artillery tower, or bastion, standing on sloping ground below and to the east of the main ridge. One of its two main gun batteries faces east along the flank of the hill and the other faces southwest enfilading the rock cut ditch between S. Girardo and Agostino. To the north of Miltiades is the Piattaforma, grandly renamed Fort Leonidas. As its Venetian name, the Platform, suggests this is a relatively simple two level gun platform standing on the northeast shoulder of the hill. Its gun batteries, now demolished, consisted of four embrasures facing southeast and two firing northeast over the narrow approach to the town below. Both of these works are protected by the eastern batteries of S. Girardo. Screen walls connect the Piattaforma to both S. Girardo and the gate complex now known as Fort Epaminondas but these cannot be considered to be part of a conventional curtain wall.

The successive flights of steps that form the direct route from the lower town to the Palamidi heights are protected first by the artillery tower known to the Venetians as the Maschio and then by the massive screen wall that climbs the slope from this tower to the rear of S. Girardo. The Maschio tower is equipped with gun embrasures covering both the north flank of the hill towards the Piattaforma and the outer face of the screen wall.

The Maschio (Fort Robert) and the approach from the town

The stepped path from the lower town to the upper fortress now starts at street level close to the northeastern tip of the Grimani bastion. It runs south before making a right angle turn east, uphill. This section is part of the original stairway, built before the construction of the Palamidi forts, leading to the entrance to the north rampart, Galerie S. Paolo (Plan 10, 1). Originally it ran directly from the dry ditch below the east face of the Grimani bastion but the lower section was destroyed when the modern road was constructed. The steps reach an arched opening in the battered wall that blocks off the western end of the rampart. Through the arch the stepped path turns south towards the southern caponier, Galerie S. Giovanni (Plan 10, 2), before turning east again to follow a zig-zag course directly uphill. Another lost stepped path that ran a little below its modern counterpart led to the arched lower entrance of S. Giovanni. The stairway, now relatively narrow, continues past the top of the caponier. From this point it is built against the cliff face with several sections carried on arches over the

Palamidi Fortifications

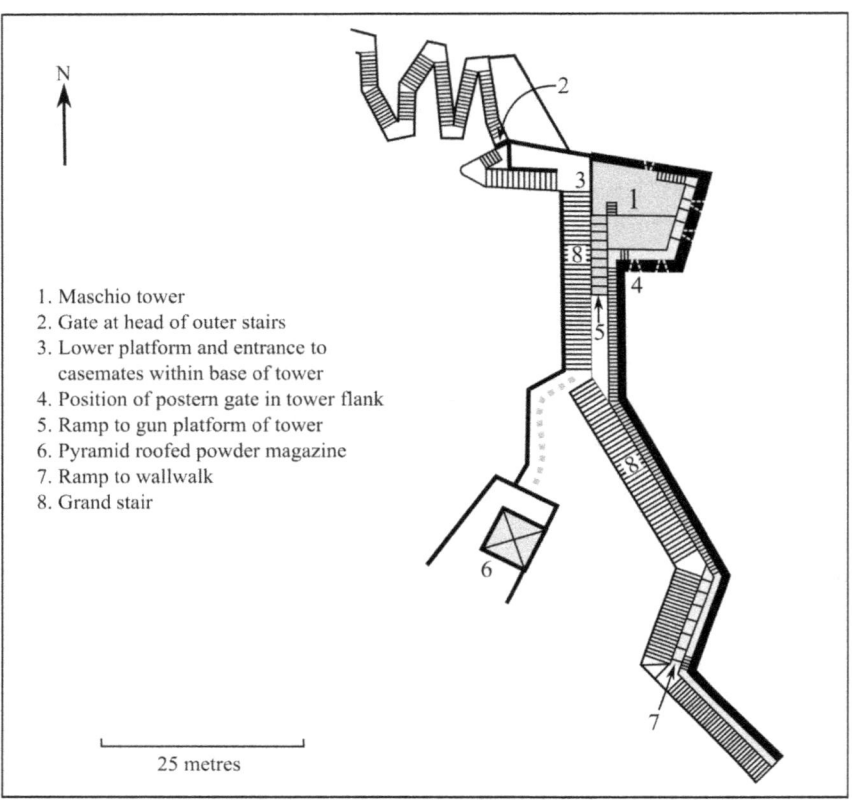

1. Maschio tower
2. Gate at head of outer stairs
3. Lower platform and entrance to casemates within base of tower
4. Position of postern gate in tower flank
5. Ramp to gun platform of tower
6. Pyramid roofed powder magazine
7. Ramp to wallwalk
8. Grand stair

Plan 11 The Maschio (Fort Robert).

irregular rocks. Eventually the stairs reach a small landing protected by a wall on its left flank from where a straight flight of steps leads to an arched gate set in a wall projecting from the base of the northwest corner of the Maschio tower (Plan 11,2). This is the lower entrance to the wide walkway communicating with the main fortifications above. The stairs beyond the gate climb to a terrace at the foot of the tower. The corbelled base of a stone sentry box projects from the northwest corner of this terrace and overlooks the approach to the gate below.

The Maschio, a name often applied in Italian to a major tower or keep, is simply a massive quadrangular tower forming the lower terminus of the long wall protecting the broad stairway to the main fortifications. The base of the tower contains two vaulted casemates. Access is via an arched doorway opening from the lower terrace into the northern casemate. This is now closed with a gate and inaccessible.

Fig. 4.1 The lower gate below the Maschio tower. Note the base of the sentry box projecting from the terrace above.

Fig. 4.2 Maschio tower: Exterior face. The splayed gun ports and the blocked up postern gate in the flank are visible.

Palamidi Fortifications

Fig. 4.3 The screen wall connecting the Maschio tower to the left and Bastione S. Girardo to the right.

Both the tower and the ascending wall are built throughout of the same heavily mortared rubble masonry. The northeast corner of the tower is reinforced with massive rusticated blocks and there is a square string course around the three external faces at the base of the parapet. A postern gate, reached from the casemates but now blocked up, is set in the tower's southern wall close against the outer face of the ascending wall. The casemate vaults support an artillery platform stepped on two levels, open at the rear but with a double parapet on the other three sides. The lower level of the parapet is pierced by arched gun ports that splay out to wide exterior openings. Two of these gun ports face south to flank the outer face of the ascending wall, two face east and one north. The great height of the tower ensures command of the ground to the east. Arches support a wall walk above the gun ports, stepped to accommodate the slope on which the tower stands and accessed by steps set against the north wall. The plain upper parapet is pierced by square loopholes for small arms. An opening

Palamidi Fortifications

Fig. 4.4 The Maschio tower: Gun ports framed by the arches supporting the wall walk above.

in the platform floor gave access to the casemate below, presumably to allow supplies to be hauled up. The tower appears to have been built in sections with long vertical joints in the masonry. Access to the platform is by a ramp leading up from the first flight of the grand stair.

The wall walk of the screen wall is directly connected with that of the Maschio tower and is stepped for much of its length. The wall's plain parapet is pierced by loopholes for small arms on two levels. The upper row of apertures, square on the inner face but tapering to a narrow vertical slit externally, is at the normal height for a defender standing on the walkway. The lower row is close to the base of the parapet. The apertures are angled steeply downwards to cover the ground near the foot of the wall. There is a further row of square loopholes below the wall walk which can only have been used if a wooden walkway had projected from the wall. Two rows of putlog holes beneath these slits indicate that such a wooden structure was planned but it is not known if it was ever built. The wall rises until it connects with the rear of the S. Girardo bastion. The upper sections of the wall walk are built without steps and lead directly onto the rear platform of the bastion.

The broad stairway at the foot of the wall rises in four flights separated by small landings. At the first landing, twenty five metres from the Maschio tower, a terrace on the right, supported by a retaining

Palamidi Fortifications

Fig 4.5 The powder magazine.

Fig 4.6 The upper gate at the head of the ascending wall and stairs.

wall built over the cliffs, leads to a powder magazine constructed on a level platform cut into the hillside. Similar to the magazine still standing on Acronauplia below, the square structure is built with the standard Venetian heavily vaulted pyramid roof. The magazine is enclosed by a low wall with a gate set between pyramid capped pillars. The iron shutters over the small openings in the magazine's walls are still in place. At the third landing of the stairway a ramp, built against the wall and supported on arches, provides another route up to the wall walk. The stairway ends at the head of the fourth flight where a right turn along a short corridor beneath the retaining wall of the Piazza d'Armi reaches the upper gate set in a plain archway (Plan 12, 1). Both this gate and its counterpart below the Maschio tower were probably only intended to control access to the fortifications from the town.

Bastione S. Girardo (Fort Andreas)

The Venetians seem to have regarded the S. Girardo bastion, the Maschio tower and the connecting wall and stair as one defensive unit.[6] This is reflected in their physical layout with the open northwest face of S. Girardo forming one corner of the Piazza d'Armi. Here the bastion's external gates, passages into its internal courtyard and the wall walk ascending from the Maschio tower all meet. The parade ground is roughly quadrangular. It is bounded by the final section of the ascending wall to the east, a steeply sloping rampart with a stepped wall walk and infantry parapet to the south (Plan 12, 6), and simple retaining walls to the north and west. The area now contains a number of modern structures. From the upper gate (Plan 12, 1) the path turns south across the Piazza then east through a final arched gate, which may be a later addition.[7]

The square tower to the right of this entrance forms a gate chamber entered by an arched opening in its east face. A postern gate in the south face of the tower (Plan 12, 3) leads via a terrace on the western side of S. Girardo to the S. Agostino bastion further south. Beyond the postern tower two flights of steps ascend to a terrace that wraps around the entire north side of the body of the fort. This forms a continuous walkway from the roof of the postern tower to the platform of the north demi-bastion and originally also gave access to the wall walk of the ascending wall from the Maschio. An archway in the wall at the rear of the terrace opens into the interior courtyard of the fort (Plan 12, 5). Ahead, beyond the stairway, are two further arched openings at ground level. The arch to the right (Plan 12, 4) provides another

Palamidi Fortifications

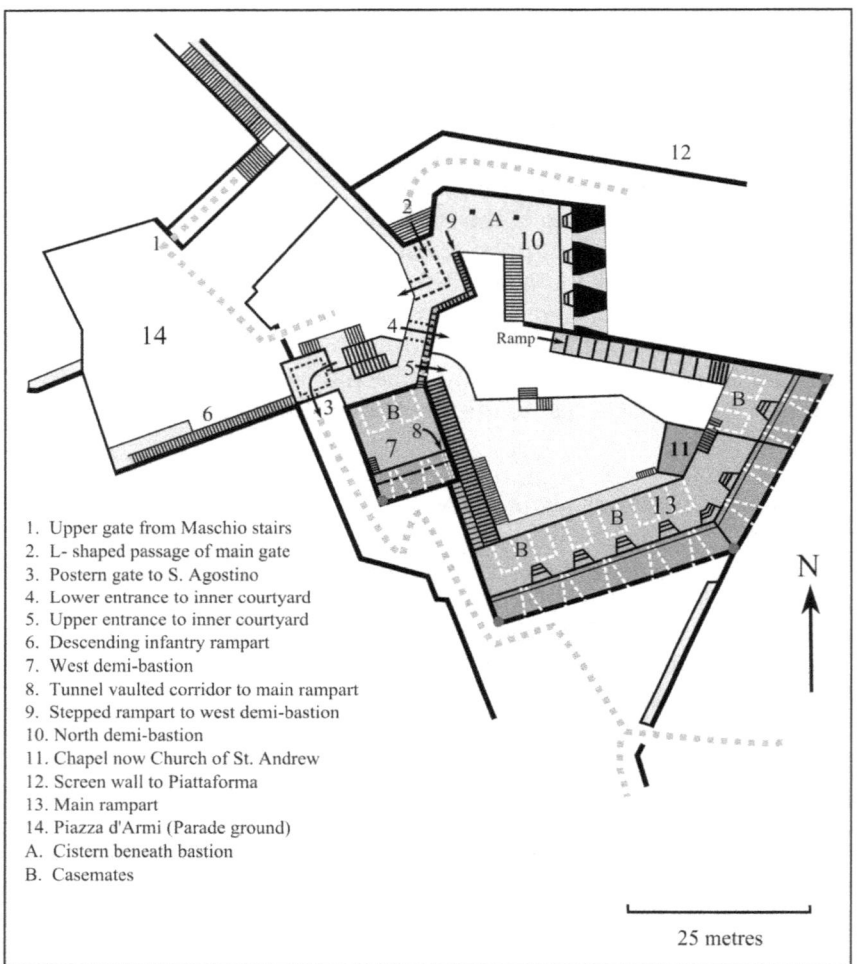

1. Upper gate from Maschio stairs
2. L- shaped passage of main gate
3. Postern gate to S. Agostino
4. Lower entrance to inner courtyard
5. Upper entrance to inner courtyard
6. Descending infantry rampart
7. West demi-bastion
8. Tunnel vaulted corridor to main rampart
9. Stepped rampart to west demi-bastion
10. North demi-bastion
11. Chapel now Church of St. Andrew
12. Screen wall to Piattaforma
13. Main rampart
14. Piazza d'Armi (Parade ground)
A. Cistern beneath bastion
B. Casemates

Plan 12 Bastione S. Girardo (Fort Andreas).

entrance to the fort's interior. The opening to the left leads into the L-shaped stepped passage of the main gate of the bastion (Plan 12, 2). The paved route to this gate from the main entrance within Fort Epaminondas to the southwest, first skirts the eastern flank of S.Girardo before entering a narrow corridor between the north demi-bastion and the adjacent screen wall. The gate is concealed behind the shoulder of the bastion at the head of a short flight of steps. The outer face is an arch of massive, smooth faced blocks surmounted by a large relief of the Lion of St Mark. The defences of the vaulted gate passage

Fig. 4.7 S. Girardo bastion: The northwest face. To the right are the steps leading to the upper terrace. Centre is the lower entrance into the inner courtyard. Top right is the upper entrance. Left is the arched passage to the main gate.

Fig 4.8 S. Girardo bastion: The west demi-bastion from the south. To the left the descending rampart forming the southern edge of the Piazza d'Armi. Note the double row of loopholes.

Fig. 4.9 S. Girardo bastion: Main gate.

included a portcullis, a murder hole in the roof above and loopholes in the end wall to allow fire down the length of the passage from the interior courtyard of the bastion. The 19C bell tower of the Church of St. Andrew now stands on the parapet above the gate.

The main body of the S. Girardo fort consists of a massive V-shaped artillery rampart, facing southeast, connected by high screen walls to subsidiary demi-bastions to the north and west. The north demi-bastion flanks the north face of the fort and commands the ground to the east which slopes down to the Piattaforma on the northeast shoulder of the hill. The west demi-bastion enfilades the western face of the fort and covers the approach to the postern gate. The walls are constructed of rubble masonry below the square sectioned string course at the level of the gun platform, with a brick artillery parapet above. Externally the corners of the fort are reinforced with massive, rusticated blocks, a technique used throughout the Palamidi fortifications. On the main rampart and the west demi-bastion artillery was deployed in arched and splayed gun ports, nine in the main battery and two on the demi-bastion. Three open embrasures were used on the north demi-bastion. Above the arched gun ports of the main rampart is a separate infantry platform with a plain parapet in rubble masonry pieced by square loopholes. Steps between each of the gun ports provide access to the infantry positions. Brick sentry boxes were mounted at each external angle of the work. Those of the main rampart can still be seen while only the bases of those on the demi-bastions survive. Both the eastern arm of the main artillery platform and the interior courtyard are stepped to accommodate the sloping

Fig. 4.10 S. Girardo bastion: Aerial view from the north. In the right foreground is the Piazza d'Armi. Centre foreground is the main gate at the rear of the north demi-bastion. The row of open casemates below the main rampart can be seen.

Fig. 4.11 S. Girardo bastion: The interior from the platform of the north demi-bastion. To the left is the stairway climbing to the main gun platform. To the right are the musketry loopholes of the western screen wall facing into the interior of the fort.

Fig. 4.12 S. Girardo bastion: The north screen wall and ramp.

ground. Barrel vaulted casemates are built within the thickness of the rampart. Now open faced, they were originally walled and equipped with doors and windows.[8] The casemates in the eastern arm of the rampart housed the fort's chapel and the residence of the priest. Access to the gun platform level is by a ramp built against the north screen wall. A flight of stairs built against the west demi-bastion and the connecting screen wall provided a second means of access. Both the ramp and stairs are carried on arches. Those supporting the stairway were also originally walled-up to provide further accommodation.

Shallow steps rise from the lowest level of the courtyard to the platform of the north demi-bastion. Within the bastion is a large cistern placed at the lowest point of the fort. Its water was accessible from draw holes in the platform above. The cistern was filled by the winter rains, collected from every surface of the fort's interior by a simple system of channels. At the western end of the north demi-bastion platform the stepped wall walk of the west screen wall rises in a dog-leg course to the higher platform of the west demi-bastion (Plan 12, 9). The parapet here is reversed; its musketry loopholes point into the

Fig. 4.13 S. Girardo bastion: View looking north from the upper terrace of the courtyard. The upper and lower passages from the Piazza d'Armi are visible. The loopholes firing into the main gate chamber can be seen below the arched gunport that allowed fire from the platform of the north demi-bastion into the courtyard.

Fig. 4.14 S. Girardo bastion: Overall view from the southeast. To the left is the loop-holed wall of Fort Themistokles.

interior of the fort. Other loopholes and gun ports face into the courtyard from the external terrace and from the north demi-bastion. These features seem to have been constructed in the belief that, in the event of the interior of the bastion being overrun, the retreating garrison would still be able to offer resistance. The gun platform of the west demi-bastion is connected to the main rampart by a tunnel vaulted passage leading beneath the brick parapet to shallow steps parallel to the main west staircase. (Plan 12, 8 and Fig. 4.11, top left). The demi-bastion also houses two vaulted casemates. These open onto the external terrace rather than the interior of the fort.

Mezzo-baloardo S. Agostino (Fort Themistokles)

The S. Agostino bastion encloses the long narrow ridge that rises to the south of S. Girardo. It consists of a massive gun platform at the highest point of the ridge connected by long walls to the flanks of S. Girardo. The western wall runs along the cliff edge and is a continuation of the retaining wall of the terrace beneath S. Girardo's western demi-bastion. For most of its length it is simply a low, plain wall forming a revetment to the levelled ground within the bastion. The cliffs below were presumably regarded as sufficient protection on this side of the work. The eastern wall however is essentially one long loopholed

Palamidi Fortifications

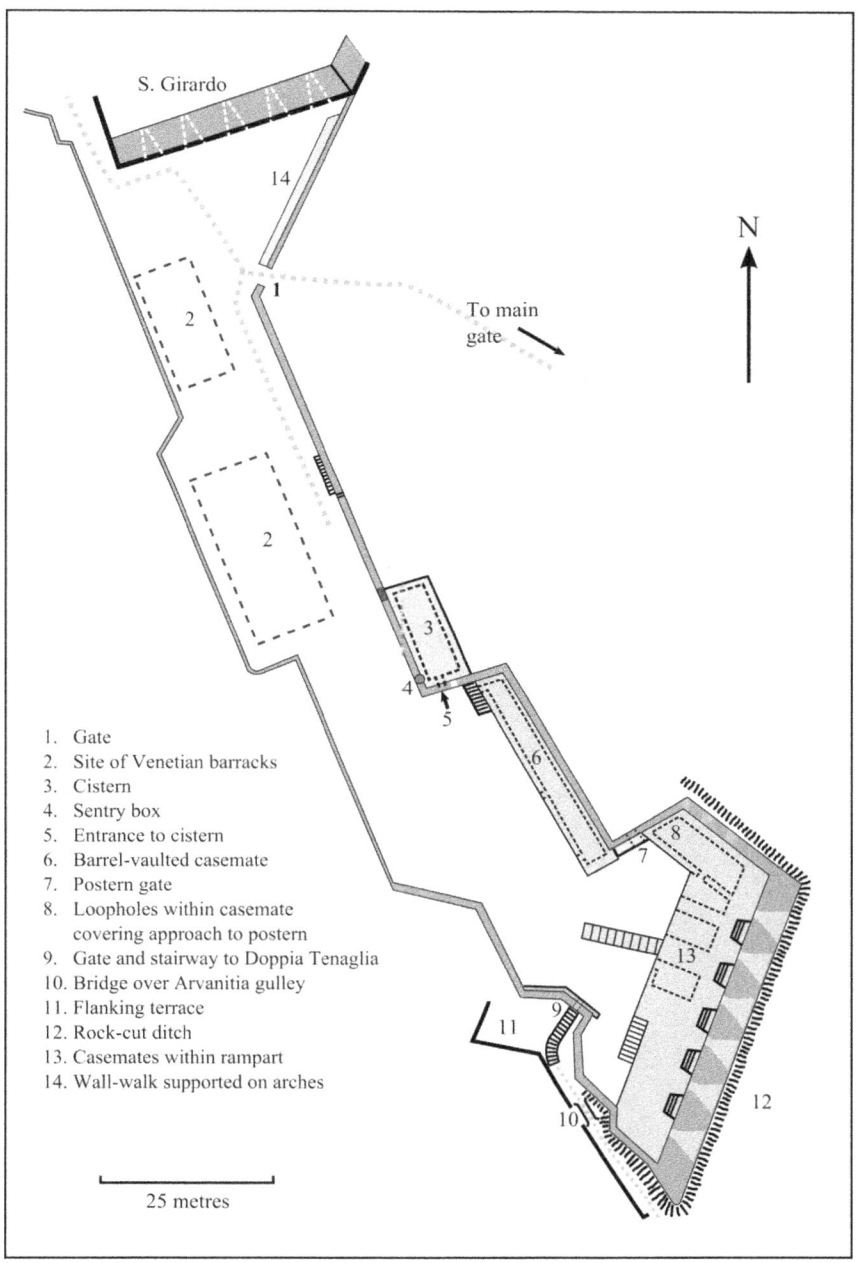

1. Gate
2. Site of Venetian barracks
3. Cistern
4. Sentry box
5. Entrance to cistern
6. Barrel-vaulted casemate
7. Postern gate
8. Loopholes within casemate covering approach to postern
9. Gate and stairway to Doppia Tenaglia
10. Bridge over Arvanitia gulley
11. Flanking terrace
12. Rock-cut ditch
13. Casemates within rampart
14. Wall-walk supported on arches

Plan 13 Mezzo-baloardo S. Agostino (Fort Themistokles).

Fig. 4.15 S. Agostino bastion: The eastern flanks.

Fig. 4.16 S. Agostino bastion: The interior of the east wall. The difference in height between exterior and interior can be clearly seen. Steps lead onto the flat wall top.

Palamidi Fortifications

infantry rampart approximately one metre thick and between three and four metres in height on its inner side. Externally the wall also forms a revetment to the slope of the ridge and at its southern end rises to a considerable height. In common with the S. Girardo bastion and the fortifications generally, the walls are battered below the level of the square section string course. At its northern end, where the wall turns northeast to connect to the salient angle of S. Girardo's southern rampart, a plain arched gate (Plan 13, 1) provides a route to the eastern fortifications and the main gate within Fort Epaminondas. The wall is predominantly of rubble masonry but the loopholes for small arms are built within a narrow band of brick a few courses deep. For most of its length the loopholes are accessible from ground level. The exception is the section north of the gate. Here a wall walk supported on arches was needed where the wall is built across a depression.

South of the gate the outlines of two level platforms mark the positions of the two-storey Venetian barrack blocks demolished in the 1950s. Ascending the slope beyond, the path first passes a vaulted cistern built against the exterior of the wall in the angle formed where it makes a wide jog to the east.[9] A platform with a thin, high parapet pierced by loopholes now stands above the vault. A draw hole is visible

Fig. 4.17 S. Agostino bastion: Steps descend to the cistern entrance beneath the arch to the left. To the right steps ascend to the roof of the barrel vaulted casemate.

in the centre of the platform. The entire structure must post-date the east wall as the original loopholes for small arms in this wall, now blocked by the mass of the cistern roof, can still be seen. (Plan 13, 3; Figs. 4.16 and 4.17) An hexagonal brick-built sentry box now stands isolated on the flat wall top. Beyond the cistern a long barrel vaulted corridor or casemate supporting a wide platform above is built against the interior of the east wall (Plan13, 6). External stairs at the northern end give access to the platform which has a plain parapet to the north and east. Three low, arched doorways at ground level open into the casemate which is equipped not only with loopholes for small arms in the external wall but also in the opposite face so that fire could be directed into the interior of the bastion.

The L-shaped gun platform that occupies the southernmost section of the fort forms a demi bastion with only one true flank. For this reason the fort was known to the Venetians as the Mezzo-baloardo S. Agostino. Its position at the highest point of the Palamidi ridge was designed to command the level ground to the south enclosed by the outwork of the Doppia Tenaglia. An impressive rock cut ditch separates the gun platform from the outwork. The main battery consists of

Fig. 4.18 S. Agostino bastion: The brick built embrasures of the main battery above the northwest face of the rock cut ditch.

Fig. 4.19 S. Agostino bastion: The interior of the southern gun platform. The arched entrances to the casemates are visible.

Fig. 4.20 S. Agostino bastion: The entrance arch to the east postern gate. Above are the loopholes defending the approach.

Fig. 4.21 S. Agostino bastion: The monolithic lintel and jambs framing the exterior of the east postern gate.

six brick built embrasures three metres deep facing southeast. These enfilade the east face of the Tenaglia as well as commanding its interior. Brick firing steps between the embrasures allowed small arms fire over the parapet. The shorter arm of the gun platform facing northeast is equipped with three smaller embrasures covering the slopes towards Fort Miltiades but the northwest flank is furnished only with loopholes for small arms. Vaulted casemates provided further accommodation within the platform while a ramp and stairs give access to the embrasures. A postern gate is concealed in the short section of wall that connects the long eastern wall to the gun platform (Plan 13, 7). A shallow arch at the base of the wall leads to the square opening of the gate. The arch supports a small platform that allowed fire from four loopholes to cover the approach. Further cover is provided by loopholes in the northwest face of the adjacent casemate (Plan 13, 8).

The route to the Doppia Tenaglia outwork is via a second postern gate on the western side of the enclosure a few metres to the north of the gun platform (Plan 13, 9). Concealed within a re-entrant angle of the wall, the square opening of the gate leads via an external flight of steps down to a small terrace built out over the cliffs. A short wall walk

Fig 4.22. S. Agostino: The west postern gate. The box machicolation and the loopholes angled sharply downwards are visible.

supported on an arch over the gate threshold allowed access to the parapet and box machicolation above the gate. Loopholes in this parapet on two levels are angled downwards to protect the approach to the gate. These features give the exterior of the gate a mediaeval appearance. At the base of the steps a path runs south along a walled

Fig. 4.23 S. Agostino: The defences above the west postern gate.

Fig. 4.24 The bridge over the Arvanitia gulley. To the right is the ramp into the Doppia Tenaglia enclosure.

ledge, or terrace, cut into the rocks beneath the southwest corner of the bastion. The terrace is divided into two parts by a small bridge across the head of the Arvanitia gulley (Plan 13, 10). This was clearly regarded as a weak point in the defences as immediately to the north of the steps the terrace extends out to the west to form a simple redan flanking the bridge and its approaches (Plan 13, 11). Its southern parapet is provided with two rows of loopholes. Those of the upper row are angled to cover the gulley below the bridge while those of the lower row slant steeply downhill. Beyond the bridge the terrace reaches the western end of the rock cut ditch and a ramp leads up into the northwest corner of the Doppia Tenaglia enclosure.

The Doppia Tenaglia (Fort Achilles)

The Doppia Tenaglia is large, rectangular work enclosed by long walls to the east and west and a major gun platform to the south with another rock cut ditch beyond, somewhat shallower than its northern counterpart. The name means double pincer and may refer to the shape of the south face of the gun platform when viewed as two V-shaped ramparts meeting at an acute angle in the centre. The work is completely open at the rear, separated from S. Agostino only by the rock cut ditch. Its rocky and uneven interior seems to be devoid of any structures north of the gun platform. The long, straight, east wall forms a revetment to the slope of the hill with the outer face considerably higher than the inner. For most of its length it has a plain infantry parapet with loopholes for small arms. However towards the southern gun platform the parapet doubles in thickness to two metres and is equipped with three embrasures facing northeast (Plan 14, 4). At its northern end the wall meets the rampart that climbs uphill from the main gate within Fort Epaminondas. This rampart runs along the edge of the counterscarp of the rock cut ditch to join the east wall at a domed sentry box (Plan 14, 3). The ramp from the S. Agostino ditch leads to the northern end of the west wall at the point where it forms a demi-bastion with its flank facing south (Plan 14, 2). A single gun embrasure faces southwest towards the sea while the parapet of the flank has a row of musketry loopholes enfilading the wall to the south. These defences were presumably thought necessary as the slopes below the west wall are slightly more accessible than those below S. Agostino. For the same reason loopholes are provided along the full length of the west wall. The string course in this section of wall, and around the outer face of the demi-bastion, consists of four courses of

Palamidi Fortifications

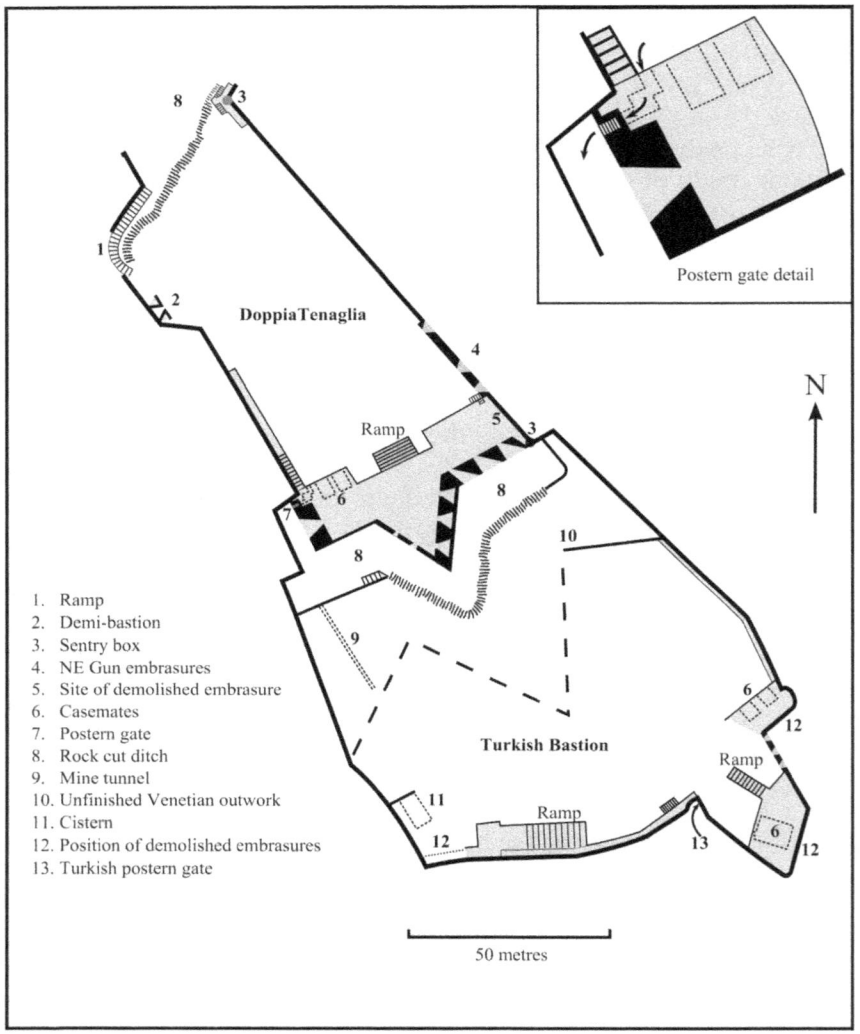

1. Ramp
2. Demi-bastion
3. Sentry box
4. NE Gun embrasures
5. Site of demolished embrasure
6. Casemates
7. Postern gate
8. Rock cut ditch
9. Mine tunnel
10. Unfinished Venetian outwork
11. Cistern
12. Position of demolished embrasures
13. Turkish postern gate

Plan 14 The Doppia Tenaglia (Fort Achilles) and the Turkish bastion (Fort Phokion).

brick. At the southern end of the west wall steps from the low wall walk lead up to the main gun platform.

Despite the shape implied by the name "double pincer", this platform or rampart simply forms a long rectangle with a triangular beak, or redan, projecting from its centre. This arrangement provides a degree of flanking cover along the southern faces of the work which

Fig. 4.25 The Doppia Tenaglia: The west wall viewed from the northwest demi-bastion. In the background is the southern gun platform with its arched casemates.

Fig. 4.26 The Doppia Tenaglia gun platform. To the right the eastern sentry box and embrasures. To the left the apex of the triangular beak. Its eastern embrasures are walled up.

Palamidi Fortifications

Fig. 4.27 The Doppia Tenaglia: Western section of the gun platform.

Fig 4.28 The Doppia Tenaglia: The arched casemates within the gun platform. The half arch to the right forms the entrance to the postern gate.

Fig. 4.29 The Doppia Tenaglia: The terrace beneath the west flank of the gun platform leading into the ditch. In the background the northwest demi-bastion.

formed the original limit of the defences before the construction of the Turkish bastion. The ditch here is smaller in depth and width than that of S. Agostino. The parapet and gun embrasures show evidence of considerable repair and alteration. The seaward, western end of the platform is said to be the point where the Turks exploded a mine during the siege of 1715.[10] Repair work to the parapet in a mixture of

Fig. 4.30 The Doppia Tenaglia: The postern gate. Above are the remains of the box machicolation.

rubble and brick is evident at this point. The eastern section of the parapet appears to be the only segment to retain its gun embrasures unmodified. Those in the east face of the triangular beak still exist but walls with narrow musketry slits have been built across the outer face of the embrasure openings. The west flank of the beak has a thin parapet pierced by two small embrasures. The western section is now equipped only with musketry slits and two small brick arched gun ports. Distinguishing later Turkish work from the Venetian original is now probably impossible. A prominent stone sentry box survives at the southeast corner of the parapet. Another seems to have existed at the apex of the beak. Originally each end of the platform was equipped with a single large embrasure facing respectively east and west.[11] Only the western example survives. Access to the gun platform from the interior of the Tenaglia is by steps at either end or by a broad ramp, now in poor condition, in the centre.

Three arched, open-faced casemates are built within the western arm of the gun platform. The narrow half arch built against the west wall forms a passage into a small gate chamber. A square door in its west face overlooking the sea opens onto a steep external stairway. Above the door are the remains of a box machicolation. Like the postern gate of S. Agostino, the stairs lead down onto a terrace beneath the west flank of the gun battery and then into the ditch.

The Turkish Bastion (Fort Phokion)

After the Ottoman re-conquest of 1715 the Turks addressed the remaining weakness of the Palamidi defences by enclosing the final unprotected section of the ridge; the area they themselves had used to attack the walls of the Tenaglia. The bastion, now known as Fort Phokion, is the largest of the enclosures on the mountain and extends south to the point where the ground begins to slope away downhill. The Venetians themselves had clearly intended to complete a further layer of defences beyond the rock cut ditch at the southern end of the Doppia Tenaglia. They extended the length of this ditch with a masonry counterscarp at each end and began work on an outwork or ravelin. Only a section of the eastern flank was completed and today it is visible as a level earth platform beyond the ditch with a masonry retaining wall (Plan 14, 10). This was subsequently incorporated into the Turkish walls. The Venetians also seem to have completed a countermine beneath the area that would have formed the western part of the outwork (Plan 14, 9). Its arched entrance portal is still visible within

Palamidi Fortifications

Fig. 4.31 Aerial view of the Turkish bastion and the southern end of the Doppia Tenaglia. In the centre foreground is the unfinished Venetian outwork.

Fig. 4.32 Fort Phokion: The unfinished Venetian outwork.

Fig. 4.33 Fort Phokion: The entrance to the counter mine,

the counterscarp wall. Access to the interior of the bastion is via a ramp, now a ruin, from the ditch floor. The Ottoman walls follow the same pattern as their Venetian counterparts forming revetments to the slope of the hill. Their plain uncrenellated parapets are furnished with narrow loopholes. The only structure visible within the enclosure is an isolated underground cistern on the western side. The square entrance door, originally gated, opens onto two flights of steps which lead down to the water level. The finely plastered interior is in good condition. There is also a draw hole in the vaulted roof.

Although the bastion's main defences are concentrated, like those of the Venetian works, at the southern end of the enclosure they lack the symmetry of the Venetian designs. Separate gun platforms were built at the southwest and southeast corners of the enclosure and an irregular shaped projecting extension of the circuit was built out over the slope of the hill to the south. This structure forms a separate bastion in its own right and has a third gun platform at its tip. The southwest platform was approached by a large ramp built against the southern wall. Schaefer's 1935 plan shows a gun battery of three embrasures at this point but the area is now a ruin. The southeast

Fig. 4.34 Fort Phokion: The entrance to the cistern.

Fig. 4.35 Fort Phokion: The southern tip of the bastion. The plain parapet is a later replacement.

Fig. 4.36 Fort Phokion: The postern gate.

platform houses two arched, open faced casemates and originally was equipped with two gun embrasures facing southeast. These have been replaced by a plain, modern parapet.

The projecting southern extension or bastion has three surviving gun embrasures in its east flank. The platform at its tip is accessed by a central ramp and houses enclosed casemates. Again its parapet is a plain, modern replacement although the original paving to support the guns is still in situ and indicates that there were a further three embrasures facing southeast at this point. The wall forming the western flank of this bastion north of the gun platform is equipped with loopholes on two levels, although it is no longer clear how the upper row was accessed. A simple postern gate pierces the wall where the west flank meets the long southern rampart (Plan 14, 13).

Bastione Staccato (Fort Miltiades)

The Bastione Staccato, that is, the detached bastion, is a tall, self contained pentagonal work positioned to command the eastern approaches to the fortifications. The fort has two main high level gun batteries. The east face, stepped due to the sloping ground, has five gun positions covering the open slopes below the main ridge. The south face has another five positions enfilading the eastern defences running uphill to the tip of S. Agostino. The height of the bastion ensured that grazing fire could be directed along the length of the rock cut ditch between Agostino and the Doppia Tenaglia. Although the

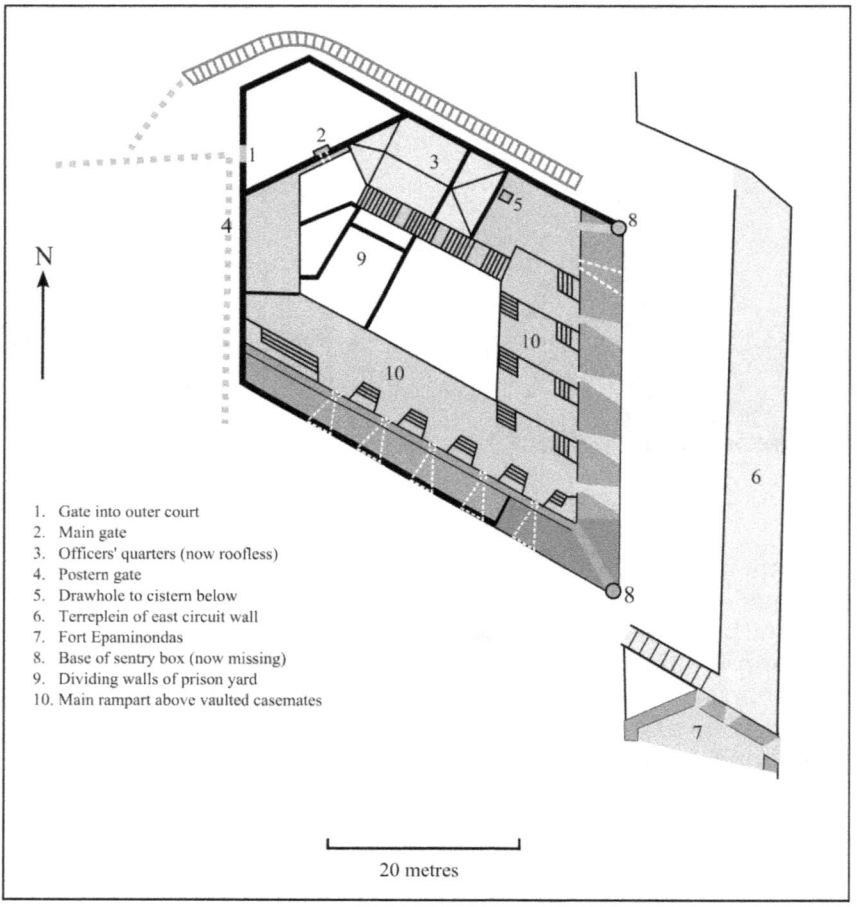

1. Gate into outer court
2. Main gate
3. Officers' quarters (now roofless)
4. Postern gate
5. Drawhole to cistern below
6. Terreplein of east circuit wall
7. Fort Epaminondas
8. Base of sentry box (now missing)
9. Dividing walls of prison yard
10. Main rampart above vaulted casemates

Plan 15 Bastione Staccato (Fort Miltiades).

Palamidi Fortifications

Fig 4.37. Bastione Staccato: Aerial view. The eight metre thick east curtain wall can be seen in the foreground. Top left is the main gate within Fort Epaminondas.

bastion is to a degree self-defensible it still relies on the adjacent works to provide flanking cover. The base of its eastern flank is protected by the outer perimeter wall a few metres to the east. This is the one part of the perimeter where a conventional thick curtain wall was employed. Behind its parapet, loopholed for small arms only, is an earth filled terreplein. This is approximately eight metres deep and is supported by an inner masonry wall.[12]

The north face of the bastion is enclosed by a low, loopholed wall forming a trapezoidal outer courtyard. The wall is pierced by a plain arched outer gate. A double box machicolation projecting from the north face of the bastion at parapet level protects the inner main gate. A small square door in the western flank of the bastion leads via an internal corridor into the rear of one of the casemates. This presumably functioned as a postern gate or sally port. The main entrance opens directly into the inner courtyard. The interior was originally one open space but is now subdivided by low internal cross walls, a relic of its use as a prison. Immediately beyond the inner gate the roofless shell of the officers' quarters can be seen on the left.[13] A long, broad

Fig. 4.38 Bastione Staccato: Outer gate to the left. Postern gate to the right. The box machicolation above the inner gate is top left.

Fig 4.39 Bastione Staccato: The casemates of the inner courtyard.

Fig 4.40 Bastione Staccato: The interior showing the cross walls dividing the courtyard. The roofless officers' quarters and the stairs to the ramparts can be seen on the right.

stairway built against the inner face of this building leads up to the level of the east gun platform. Steps from a casemate beneath the stairway descend to the bastion's cistern. Water from the cistern could be drawn from an opening in the floor of the platform above. The water collection system is clearly visible. Virtually every flat surface within the bastion incorporates a drainage channel directing rainfall into the cistern. Vaulted casemates within the ramparts surround the courtyard on four of its five sides. They retain their stone framed doors and round window openings.

The Bastione Staccato closely resembles S. Girardo in both style and materials with rubble masonry walls surmounted by massive, brick artillery parapets. The external corners are again reinforced with large rusticated blocks. The south facing rampart has the same style of deep, flared, brick arched gun ports below a separate infantry platform. Again steps between each of the gun ports give access to the infantry positions. For three quarters of its length this infantry parapet is the usual plain wall with square loopholes for small arms. Typically the loopholes have four external apertures to allow a variety of firing angles both ahead and steeply downwards to cover the approach to the wall. Each opening covers a very specific area of ground and

Fig 4.41 Bastione Staccato: The south flank.

Fig 4.42 Bastione Staccato: Detailed view of the south flank showing the depth of the main gun ports and the unusual embrasures for small arms in the upper parapet.

Fig 4.43 Bastione Staccato: The gun platform and upper infantry parapet of the south rampart.

provides almost total protection to the defender. This style of loophole is to be found throughout the fortifications. However at the southeast corner of the bastion, overlooking the main gate within Fort Epaminondas below, the infantry parapet is massively thickened in brick. Here the normal simple loophole is replaced by small, arched ports in the inner face of the parapet. These open into splayed embrasures in the outer face (Fig. 4.42). The east rampart consists of four stepped terraces and is equipped with four open embrasures and one brick arched gun port at its northern end. Two small arched ports pierce the thin parapet of the north face. Brick sentry boxes were mounted at the northeast and southeast angles of the work. Only their bases survive.

The Piattaforma (Fort Leonidas)

The Piattaforma, the platform, consists of three descending terraces built on the northeast brow of the Palamidi ridge overlooking the original approach to the town between the steep slopes of the hill and the marshes of the bay. When first built it was equipped with two gun batteries. On the upper terrace four open embrasures faced southeast to command the long eastern flank of the hill. A second battery with

Palamidi Fortifications

two embrasures at the northeast apex of the lowest terrace could bombard the approach to the town below.[14] Unfortunately all traces of these batteries have been obliterated. The terraces are supported on their northern and eastern sides by high walls or revetments. The rear of the lower terrace opens onto an irregular open court with a simple arched gate on its southern side (Plan 16, 6). The lower end of the long, loopholed screen wall descending the slope from the S. Girardo bastion forms the northern side of this enclosure. Access to the middle terrace, which retains its loopholed western parapet, is via a corridor gated at its western end (Plan 16, 7), or by steps from the upper terrace. A barrack block, now demolished, stood at the southwestern end

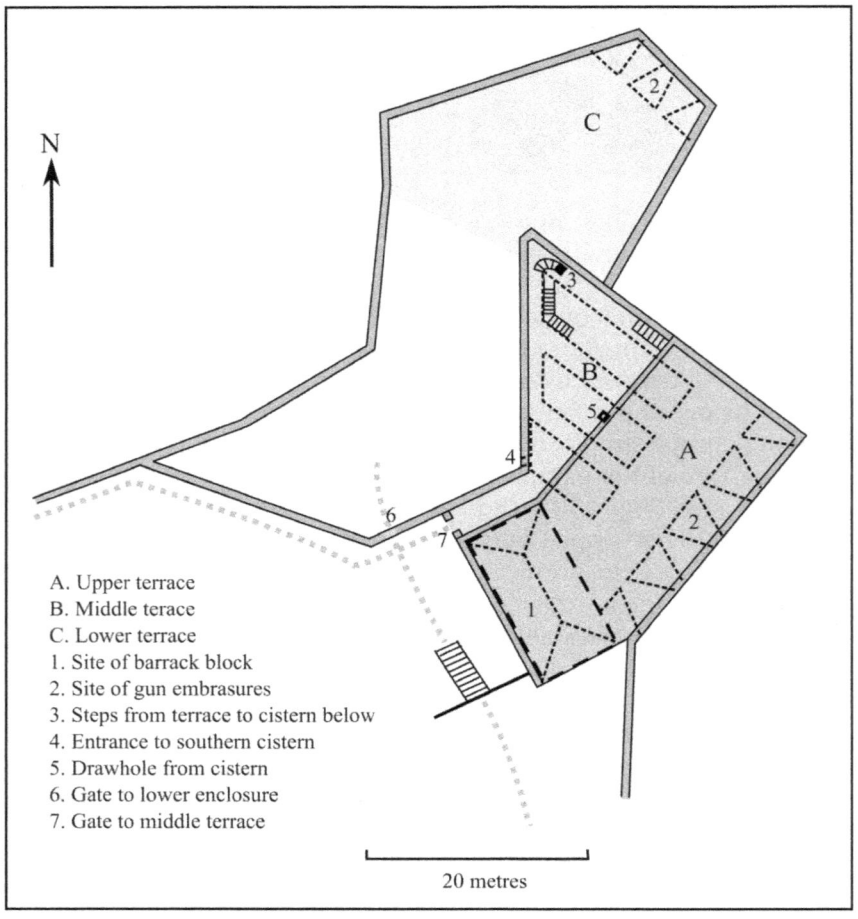

A. Upper terrace
B. Middle terace
C. Lower terrace
1. Site of barrack block
2. Site of gun embrasures
3. Steps from terrace to cistern below
4. Entrance to southern cistern
5. Drawhole from cistern
6. Gate to lower enclosure
7. Gate to middle terrace

Plan 16 The Piattaforma (Fort Leonidas).

Palamidi Fortifications

Fig. 4.44 The Piattaforma with the Bastione Staccato behind seen from the position of the original approach to the lower town.

Fig. 4.45 The Piattaforma: The upper terrace. The original parapet and gun embrasures have disappeared. The arched entrance to the lower enclosure is visible to the left.

Fig 4.46 The Piattaforma: The northern cistern. The steps lead down to water level from the arched ledge in the west wall of the middle terrace.

Fig. 4.47 The Piattaforma: The west face of the middle terrace showing the openings into the cisterns from the lower courtyard. The loopholes in the parapet of the middle terrace can be seen above.

of the upper terrace and may have served to close off the rear of the platform. This terrace is now bare and open at the rear and there is no trace of the original parapet. Another screen wall connects the southern end of the terrace to the thick curtain wall to the east of the Bastione Staccato.

Beneath the upper and middle terraces lie three massive cisterns, now dry. Although positioned at the northern edge of the fortifications in a strategically weak position, this is the lowest point of the entire site and the place where the greatest volume of rain run-off could be collected. The cisterns are partially open at their front faces and are in remarkably good condition. Access to the northern cistern is via steps descending from an opening in the surface of the middle terrace. These lead down to a platform or ledge set beneath an open arch in the west face of the middle terrace. Steps within the cistern continue to water level. The middle cistern appears to have no direct access but the three chambers are interconnected by water channels and there is a draw hole in the middle terrace above. A rectangular door in the corner of the west face of the terrace opens into the southern cistern from the lower courtyard.[15]

Fort Epaminondas

When Palamidi fell to Ottoman forces in July 1715 the main gate complex, now known as Fort Epaminondas, and the long wall connecting it to the northeast corner of the Doppia Tenaglia were unfinished. Sagredo's report of 1714 mentions his plan to complete the curtain connecting the Piattaforma and the Doppia Tenaglia and place the main gate at its centre.[16] He provides no further details of the intended construction but it is generally assumed that the Turks subsequently

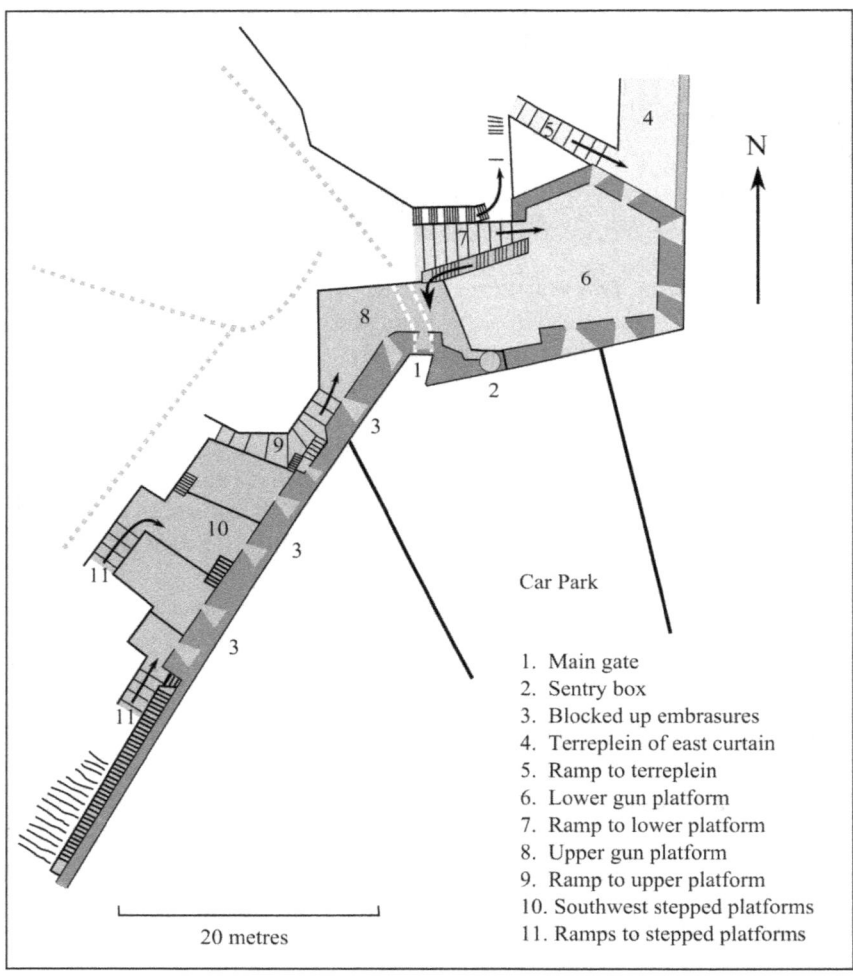

1. Main gate
2. Sentry box
3. Blocked up embrasures
4. Terreplein of east curtain
5. Ramp to terreplein
6. Lower gun platform
7. Ramp to lower platform
8. Upper gun platform
9. Ramp to upper platform
10. Southwest stepped platforms
11. Ramps to stepped platforms

Plan 17 Fort Epaminondas and the southeast defences.

Palamidi Fortifications

Fig. 4.48 Fort Epaminondas. The main gate is almost completely shielded by the projecting beak of the bastion. The gun embrasures in the parapet above the gate have been walled up.

Fig. 4.49 Fort Epaminondas. The height of bastion to the east is partially masked by the modern car park. Fort Miltiades looms behind.

Fig 4.50 Fort Epaminondas: View of the barrel vaulted bent passageway of the main gate from the interior.

completed the work to the Venetian plan. The absence of this curtain wall at the time of the Turkish siege does not seem to have affected the fortifications' defensive capability. The southeastern slopes were covered by the main gun batteries on the hill and the bastions had been carefully sited to avoid areas of dead ground. Indeed the Turks chose to attack the southern end of the Doppia Tenaglia on the highest point

Palamidi Fortifications

Fig 4.51 The irregular series of gun platforms climbing the slope to the southwest of Fort Epaminondas. The stepped parapet with its blocked up embrasures can be seen.

of the ridge and this is where they successfully exploded a mine. The southeast curtain wall as completed may even represent a change to the original plan. Certainly the simple construction and the somewhat ad hoc arrangement of the gun platforms to the southwest of the main gate does not seem typical of the Venetian designs.

The gate is housed within an irregular bastion on two levels. The five sided lower level forms a gun platform built out over sloping ground that falls away to the east. The height of the bastion on this side is masked by the terrace of the modern car park. Its northeastern face abuts the wide curtain wall to the east of Fort Miltiades approximately six metres below. The stone parapet is pierced by seven splayed embrasures on three sides of the work. Although these cover a field of fire of almost one hundred and eighty degrees they provide virtually no flanking cover along the outer faces of the adjacent walls. Access to this level of the bastion is by a broad ramp built against the inner, northern side of the work. A freestanding flight of steps leads from the lower platform to the upper, western level that houses the bent, vaulted gate passage. Roughly L-shaped, this platform has a beaked extension at its southeastern corner protecting the outer face of the gate which is set at an angle to the adjacent wall. A relief of a Turkish scimitar can be seen high up on the external wall to the left of the gate confirming that the bastion is at least partly Ottoman work.

The parapet of this platform is equipped with three gun embrasures including one directly above the gate. At some later date all three openings have been blocked up with thin walls pierced by narrow loopholes. Another substantial ramp to the south allowed artillery to be hauled up to the gun platform. A multangular sentry box is corbelled out from the southeastern corner. Vaulted casemates were constructed within both levels of the bastion with access provided by arched openings on either side of the gate passage.

The first section of the long wall connecting the gate complex to the east wall of the Doppia Tenaglia climbs the hill in a series of four stepped platforms connected by various ramps and stairs. Each of these small quadrangular structures, more crudely constructed than the main works, was equipped with a parapet containing a single open gun embrasure facing southeast to cover the approaches to the main gate. Again these embrasures are now blocked up. Southwest, beyond the platforms the wall is thinner with a plain loopholed infantry parapet and a stepped wall walk. The wall runs along the outer edge of the rock cut ditch to meet the northeast corner of the Doppia Tenaglia at a domed sentry box.

Notes

1. Gerola, *Fortificazioni*, pp. 394-395. Giaxich was the name given by the Venetians to Antun Jančić, a Dalmatian engineer, who worked on several Venetian fortresses.
   See www.jancic-project.org/en/antun-Jančić.
2. Report of Agostino Sagredo, Δελτίον Ιστορικής και Εθνολογικής Εταιρείας της Ελλάδος V, pp. 742-745. Sagredo gives a detailed account of the work completed.
3. The Venetians abandoned the mountain when a charge was detonated in a mine the Turks had dug beneath the outer wall of the Doppia Tenaglia. Although it did little damage it precipitated the garrison's flight down to the city which promptly surrendered. Benjamin Brue, *Journal de la campagne que le Grand Vesir a faite en 1715 pour La Conquête de la Morée*, pp. 28-30.
4. Αντωνιάδης Μπάμπης, «Ημερολόγια» φυλακών της πόλης του Ναυπλίου.
5. Schaefer calls this unfinished work the *Bonetto*. Schaefer, *Neue Untersuchungen*, p. 165, Fig. 3.
6. Report of Agostino Sagredo, Δελτίον V, p.742.
7. Schaefer's 1935 plan does not show this gate or the current divi-

sion of the Piazza into two levels, *Neue Untersuchungen*, p. 165, Fig. 3.
8. Kevin Andrews, *Castles of the Morea*, p. 104, Fig. 114.
9. Schaefer's plan clearly shows the structure outside the main east wall, *Neue Untersuchungen*, p. 165, Fig. 3.
10. Benjamin Brue, *Journal del campagne*, pp. 29-30: "Le 20, à six heures du matin, les Turcs firent jouer le mine que l'on avoit faite sous la tenaille, laquelle ne fit pas un grand effet, n'ayant fait sauter qu'un pan de muraille de cet ouvrage du côté de la mer, qui est escarpé."
11. Schaefer, *Neue Untersuchungen*, p. 165, Fig. 3.
12. In November 1714 Sagredo described this curtain wall as under construction. It is not clear if the work was completed by the Venetians or the Turks. Report of Agostino Sagredo, *Δελτίον V*, p.744.
13. Ibid., p.744.
14. The position of these embrasures and the barrack block on the upper terrace is shown on Schaefer's plan. *Neue Untersuchungen*, p. 165, Fig. 3.
15. The arrangement of three cisterns is at variance with Sagredo's report where he clearly states "Esso piattaforma ha quattro Casematto, et una piciola Cisterna." *Δελτίον V*, p.744. The three cisterns may represent a Turkish re-building.
16. Ibid., p.744.

5

Drepanon Fort

Although Nafplio became the capital of the Venetian Morea after 1699, its limitations as a naval base, particularly the absence of any dry dock facilities for the repair of the fleet, led the Venetians to develop the natural harbours to be found on the indented coastline to the southeast of the town. The most important of these seems to have been the almost land locked bay of Drepanon approximately twelve kilometres away. The bay forms an extended inlet, almost three kilometres long, separated from the open sea by a narrow peninsula. It provided a deep water anchorage in its outer reaches and a shallow inner section where a dry dock could be constructed. The bay was in use by 1701 when Francesco Grimani, in a report to the Venetian Senate, recommended protecting the anchorage with a fort on each side of the entrance.[1] Although plans for these forts were prepared, construction did not begin until 1714 when Agostino Sagredo built a single fort to a modified design at the end of the peninsula.[2] After the Venetian defeat in 1715 it seems to have been left to deteriorate.

The fort stands on the rocky shore at the tip of the promontory and is concealed from the seaward side by the slope of the ridge. Its main armament consists of a battery on three levels built directly on the rocks at the water's edge covering the entrance to the bay. When Kevin Andrews visited the site in the 1950s the hillside was bare but it is now so overgrown that many of the defensive features are concealed.[3] The rear of the work, to the west and north, is protected by a broad rampart with a plain parapet and wall walk. In plan the main western section forms a shallow, re-entrant, V-shape. To the south, at the highest point of the site, this terminates in a roughly D-shaped platform above the rocks of the cliff edge. At its northern end a short extension ran east to the water's edge where there was another round platform, now little more than scattered rubble.

The sea battery has three elements. At its northern end is a gun platform built over a large cistern. The parapet, facing the interior of the bay, is now almost completely missing. The middle section consists of a lower wall with three embrasures also facing the bay. These two elements stand on a platform cut into the hillside. The rear rock face of the platform, partially reinforced by a retaining wall, creates a narrow corridor four metres wide and two metres deep behind the cistern. The southern part of the battery is built at a higher level and forms a roughly rectangular bastion with embrasures in the parapet facing east into the bay and south to cover the entrance channel. A ramp connects the two levels. Access to the platform over the cistern is

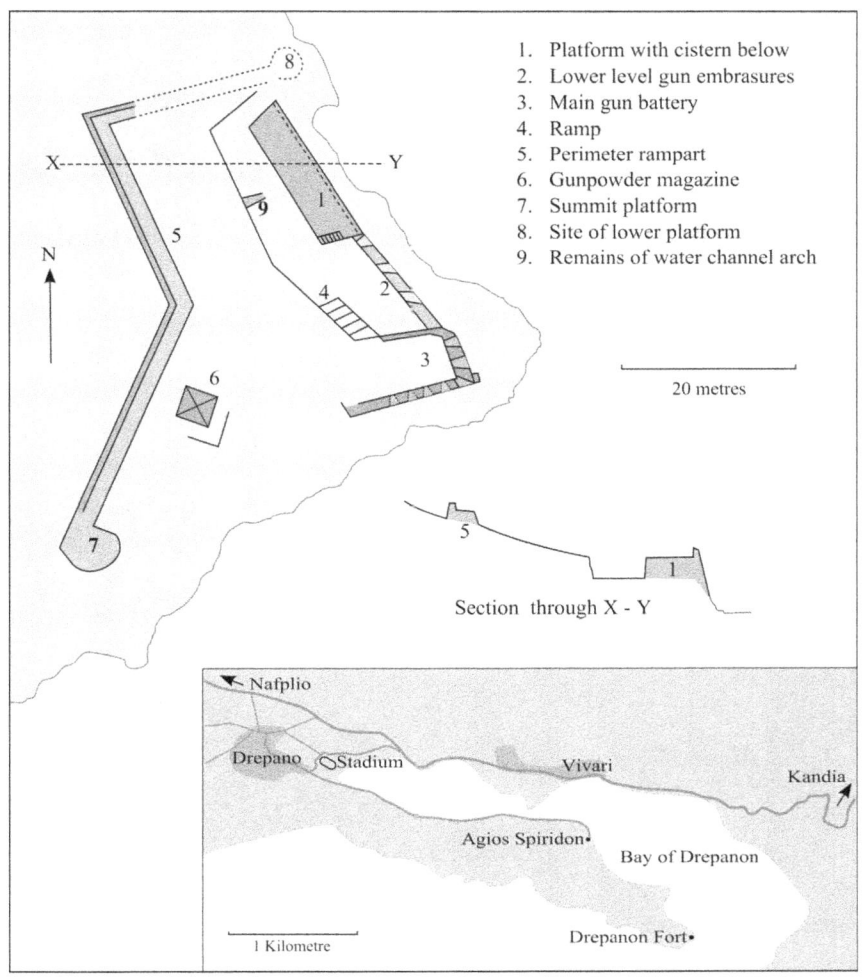

Plan 18 Drepanon Fort.

Drepanon Fort

Fig. 5.1 Drepanon Fort: The outer face of the sea battery. To the right the platform above the cistern.

Fig. 5.2 Drepanon Fort: The pyramid roof of the gunpowder magazine. The terrace on which it stands is completely overgrown.

Fig. 5.3 Drepanon Fort: The gun embrasures of the central section of the sea battery.

via steps at its southern end. The only surviving building visible within the irregular upper enclosure defined by the outer rampart is a gunpowder magazine with the typical Venetian pyramid roof, thick walls and domed interior. The building stands on a level platform cut into the hillside now almost completely overgrown with vegetation. Only the roof of the magazine is easily visible.[4]

The fort is constructed throughout of rough limestone blocks in a utilitarian style with none of the embellishments of the works on Palamidi. The size of the cistern emphasises the importance of water collection to the security of the site. Surface water run-off from the interior of the upper enclosure was collected and brought to the cistern by a channel carried on a stone arch bridging the rear corridor and discharging into the cistern through an opening in its roof. A fragment of this arch survives. The enclosure may have been at least partly paved to facilitate water collection. Access to the fort during its brief period of occupation may have been entirely by sea although there is no trace of an obvious landing place. Equally there is no visible entrance in the surrounding rampart, although one may have existed in the ruined northern arm.

Today the fort may be reached by driving from Drepano village to the church of Agios Spiridon on the southern shore of the bay. The football stadium at the eastern end of the village provides a useful landmark for locating the road to the church. The fort is a further one kilometre southeast. An initial vague footpath rapidly peters out and the greater part of the route is through difficult scrub vegetation. It is best to keep as close to the shore as possible.

Notes

1. Kevin Andrews, *Castles of the Morea*, p. 239 and Plate XXV.
2. Report of Agostino Sagredo, *Δελτίον V*, p.737.
3. Kevin Andrews, *Castles of the Morea*, p. 240, Fig. 230.
4. The area of the fort was cleared of its scrub vegetation in April 2018.

6

Castle of Thermisi

The territory of Thermisi was an important outlying possession of the Venetians at Nafplio for the century and a half of their first occupation and again during their brief second period of tenure after 1686. The origins of the castle are obscure. It may have been constructed first by the Franks some time after 1212, or it may have an earlier Byzantine foundation date.[1] It first appears in the written record in 1347 in the will of Walter II of Brienne.[2] When he died the castle passed to the d'Enghien family via the marriage of his sister Isabelle. Thermisi was sold to the Venetians along with Nafplio and Argos by Marie d'Enghien in 1388 although the Republic was not able to take possession until 1394 (see Introduction).

Turkish incursions into the territory began as early as 1397 and culminated in an all-out invasion of the Morea in 1458. The first Turko-Venetian war began in 1463 and Argos was lost that year. Hostilities continued until 1479 when peace was agreed. The area controlled by the Venetians was reduced to the southern edge of the plain of Argos and the southwest part of the Argolid peninsula. The exact line of the border remained in dispute until 1482 when Bartolomeo Minio successfully concluded extended negotiations with a series of Turkish boundary commissions and Thermisi was confirmed as a Venetian possession.[3] It remained in the hands of the Republic throughout the second war with the Turks (1499-1503) but when a third war began in 1537 the castle surrendered after nearby Kastri, modern Ermioni, was taken.[4] The subsequent Turkish occupation lasted until the Venetian re-conquest of 1686. When the Morea fell for the final time to the Turks in 1715 the site of Thermisi vanishes from the record. McLeod speculates that, along with the castle of Argos, it was blown up by the retreating Venetians.[5]

The castle of Thermisi occupies the western part of a dramatic and precipitous ridge that lies six kilometres east of Ermioni and two kilometres inland. The ridge runs from east to west for approximately

Castle of Thermisi

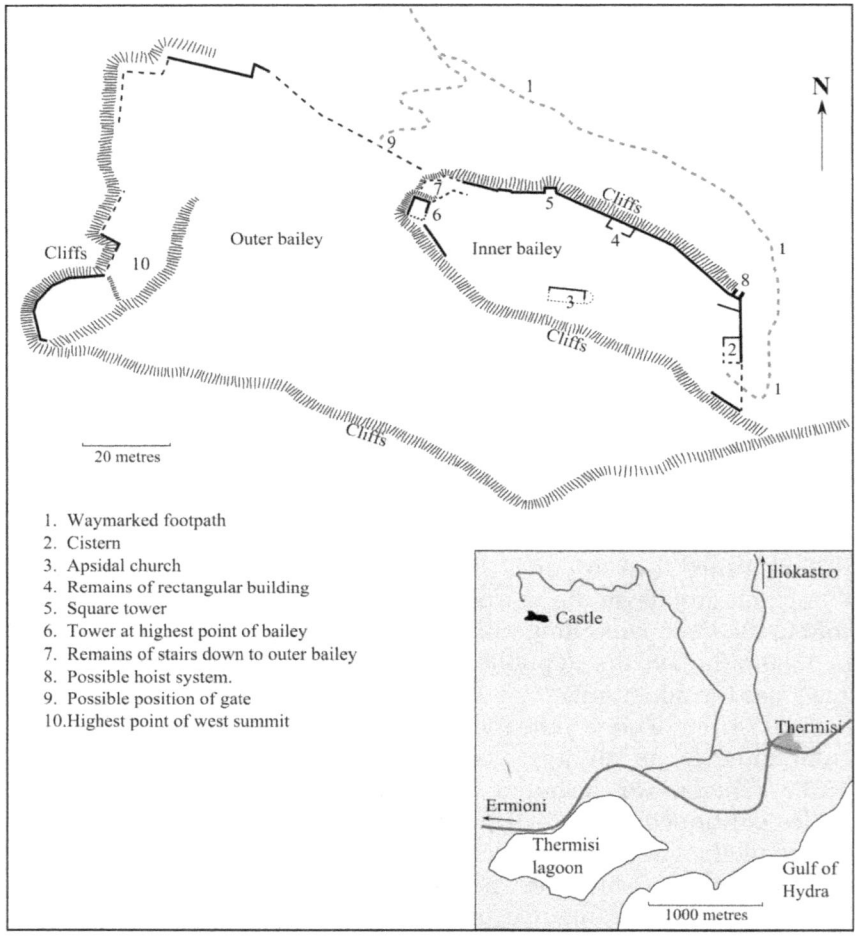

1. Waymarked footpath
2. Cistern
3. Apsidal church
4. Remains of rectangular building
5. Square tower
6. Tower at highest point of bailey
7. Remains of stairs down to outer bailey
8. Possible hoist system.
9. Possible position of gate
10. Highest point of west summit

Plan 19 Castle of Thermisi.

500m, rises to a height of 250m above the coastal plain and is almost completely encircled by cliffs. The western half of the ridge consists of two peaks separated by a saddle. The inner bailey, or acropolis, of the fortress occupies the eastern peak. The saddle and west peak form a steeply sloping outer bailey. Cliffs at the base of this slope isolate the ridge from the lower ground to the south. With these natural defences the place was believed to be impregnable and could be defended with a very small garrison. Walls were only necessary to the north, west and east of both the inner and outer circuits. The castle seems to have functioned as a place of refuge for the local population.[6] The lower

Castle of Thermisi

Fig. 6.1 Thermisi: The crags viewed from the south. The walls of the inner bailey are visible crowning the eastern peak to the right. The outer bailey occupies the western summit and the central slopes above the lower cliffs.

Fig. 6.2 Thermisi: The north wall of the outer bailey.

Castle of Thermisi

Fig. 6.3 Thermisi: The walls of the inner bailey viewed from the east. The way marked route follows a diagonal line through the rocks below to reach the breach visible at the extreme left.

courses of numerous ruined buildings can be seen within the outer bailey. However the castle's main purpose was the protection of the valuable salt pans on the coast below, an important economic asset to the Venetians.[7] After 1463 and the loss of the greater part of the plain of Argos the fertile coastal strip also became increasingly important as an agricultural resource.[8]

The castle is inaccessible from the south but a paved road, in poor condition in sections, leads inland from the coast into the valley north of the ridge. The northern cliffs are significantly lower than those to the south and access to Thermisi must always have been from this side. The road ends in a parking area. From here a path, way marked with large red arrows, leads first east beneath the cliffs, then south climbing a cleft in the rocks to reach a breach in the east wall of the inner bailey. Over ten metres of the curtain wall is missing here and it is now impossible to determine if this represents an original entry point. If a gate did exist it would have been inaccessible to pack animals. A pair of close set buttresses at the northeast corner of the bailey may represent the location of a hoist providing a solution to this problem.[9] On entering the circuit through the breach a cistern can be seen

Castle of Thermisi

on the right built against the inner face of the east curtain wall. This location at the lowest point of the hill is the obvious point for a cistern filled by surface water collection. The eastern wall has clearly been increased in height at some point in its history, walling up the original Venetian work to create a plain flat topped parapet. The outline of the characteristic Venetian swallow tail merlons can still be made out within the masonry. The wall is now pierced by simple loopholes, square on the inner face but tapering to narrow external vertical slits.[10] Along the north wall the Venetian crenellation stands unmodified. In places the remains of a narrow wall walk survive. The lower courses of a modest building stand against the northern wall at its mid-point and a little further west there is a small, square, open faced tower.

Save for two short spur walls at the southeast and southwest corners of the circuit no fortifications were required above the southern cliffs. The partial remains of a Byzantine chapel stand on one of the few level areas of the bailey overlooking these cliffs. Only the north wall and a fragment of the apse with its distinctive stone and tile

Fig. 6.4 Thermisi: The northeast corner of the inner bailey with a section of the surviving Venetian crenellation. The twin buttresses that may have supported a hoist are visible to the left.

Fig. 6.5 Thermisi: The apse of the Byzantine chapel.

decoration survive intact. A tower, or small keep, a mere six metres by five metres in size, stood at the highest, western point of the bailey. Again only fragments of its walls survive. Immediately north of the tower, at the northwest corner of the bailey, are the remains of a series of descending terraces which seem to have formed part of a stairway leading down to the saddle below. The lower section is now missing and the route ends abruptly above a vertical cliff. There is therefore now no direct access between the inner and outer baileys.[11]

To reach the outer bailey and western peak it is necessary to retrace one's steps to a point where an indistinct track leads up through the

Castle of Thermisi

Fig 6.6 Thermisi: The inner bailey from the west. To the right the fragments of the tower or keep. To the left the possible remains of stairs descending to the outer bailey.

rocks to the lowest point of the saddle (Plan 19, 9). Entry here is through the eastern section of the north wall which has been almost completely demolished. The debris of the wall's rubble masonry litters the northern slopes below. Although no evidence for a gate can now be seen this is the only possible location for an entrance although again the there is no easy approach from the valley below. The line of the northern wall begins at the foot of the inner bailey cliff, crosses the saddle and climbs the western heights in a series of steps. At its western end it stands to its full height and preserves its plain parapet and stepped wall walk. The line of the west wall can be traced for most of its length along the cliff edge. At the southwest corner of the circuit the wall terminates in another well preserved section that curves around a projecting rocky spur. Again no walls were required above the southern cliffs. The interior of the bailey contains the foundations of a

Fig. 6.7 Thermisi: The southwest corner of the outer bailey.

surprising number of collapsed or demolished buildings and is littered with fallen blocks. Heavily mortared rubble masonry was used throughout the castle.

Thermisi had a well deserved reputation for impregnability but this must have been at the expense of difficult access. An adequate water supply must also have been a problem. Whatever the origins of the castle the surviving walls seem to date entirely from the first period of Venetian occupation with later repairs and modifications by the Turks.[12] There is no evidence of any work from the second Venetian period. The complete demolition of a section of the east wall of the inner bailey and the eastern part of the north wall of the outer bailey gives some credence to the idea that they were blown up by the retreating Venetians.

Notes

1. The remains of a Byzantine chapel stand within the inner bailey of the castle. This has been tentatively dated to the 11th or 12th century. Of course the chapel may pre-date the construction of any defences. Mccleod, *Kiveri and Thermisi,* p. 388 note 41.
2. Ibid., p. 379.

3. Diana Wright, *Dispacci from Nauplion*, pp. 239-243.
4. Kastri was another walled settlement during the first period of Venetian occupation but virtually no traces of its walls now survive. Mccleod, *Kiveri and Thermisi,* pp. 381-382 and note 13.
5. Mccleod, *Kiveri and Thermisi*, p. 382.
6. In a dispatch of 1480 Minio reported that with the threat of Ottoman attacks he had given instructions to the local inhabitants to retreat to the castle. Diana Wright, *Dispacci from Nauplion*, p. 15.
7. Diana Wright, *Dispacci from Nauplion*, p. 21; Mccleod, *Kiveri and Thermisi*, p. 381.
8. Diana Wright, *Dispacci from Nauplion*, pp. 21 and 33.
9. MacLeod calls this feature a pulley entrance. Mccleod, *Kiveri and Thermisi*, p. 388.
10. This type of modification was a common Turkish practice and belongs to the period after 1537. Walled up Venetian crenellations can be seen as far afield as the castle of Old Navarino, (Andrews, *Castles of the Morea*, p. 44), and Nafpaktos, (Brooks, *Castles of Northwest Greece*, p. 32).
11. The crags of Thermisi are now used by rock climbers and a metal ladder and wire ropes provide a hazardous route down this cliff.
12. Mccleod, *Kiveri and Thermisi*, p. 389.

7

Summary

Nafplio's role as a port arose from its natural sheltered position and shallow beach suitable for loading. The gradual silting of the bay might, in other circumstances, have led to the abandonment of the site for a more usable location but the investment over the centuries in the fortifications and infrastructure of the town created a situation of geographic inertia in which further investment, for example in dredging, was used to extend the useful life of the port. Nafplio during the first Venetian occupation was a way station, never a naval base. Only towards the end of the second occupation were maintenance facilities developed, at Nafplio itself and nearby at Drepanon.

For centuries Nafplio possessed a position of natural strength as its protracted resistance to the armies of the Franks proved. The Republic of Venice acquired Nafplio at the end of the14C at the point where urban fortifications were beginning to adapt to the threat of gunpowder weapons. Initially the Venetians simply repaired the mediaeval defences they had inherited making minor improvements when possible. The addition of small gun ports to the round towers of the mediaeval walls may have been their first adaptation. An example survives at the tower near the Gate of the Grotto. Serious modernisation of the defences began after 1470 and the Venetian military engineers used every technique then available against gunpowder artillery. On the north and east sides of the Castle of the Franks the walls were modified to deflect gunshot by adding a massive sloping talus. With the construction of the new defensive line, known as the Gambello traverse, the technique used was to place an advance wall, or faussebraye, in front of the main wall to mask the base from fire. New gates were constructed in protected positions concealed in the flanks of the defences. The outer line of defence on the acropolis was moved eastwards by the construction of Castel del Toro, and the Castle of the Rock was built to defend the harbour. The walls of both the lower town and the acropolis were given an offensive capability by the addition of

Summary

gun batteries. Initially these were housed in small arched embrasures set below a conventional crenellated parapet or in open embrasures on the roof of a tower.[1] Subsequent rebuilding after 1500 produced larger tapered embrasures for heavier calibre weapons and ballistic shaping of the parapets. Although some of the important positions were still occupied by round towers, the Contarina tower and the salient of Castel del Toro for example, detached works and flanking batteries had also begun to appear by the time the Republic ceded the town to the Turks in 1540. Examples are the detached battery of the Marina and the ravelin at the head of the land front ditch.

The fortifications of the castle of Thermisi must have been repaired or rebuilt in the early part of the first Venetian occupation. Thereafter the castle seems to have remained untouched. The adaptations for artillery that began to appear at Nafplio were never applied at Thermisi while the brief period of the second Venetian occupation passed it by. Consequently the surviving sections of parapet with their characteristic swallow tail merlons provide a snapshot of the appearance of Venetian fortification before artillery modifications.

By the time of the second Venetian occupation of Nafplio the *trace italienne* had become the standard for urban fortification and the new land front constructed by the Republic to protect the lower town followed this form as far as the peculiarities of the topography would allow. Thus the slope of the land made it necessary to build the Grimani bastion in ascending terraces and the additional detached Mocenigo battery had to be constructed due to silting of the bay. The monumental appearance of the new works was both functional and an architectural statement of the town's status as the capital of the Morea. During this period the Venetians moved their military barracks and magazines to the western end of the acropolis in an attempt to place these resources beyond the range of any guns positioned on the Palamidi heights. However Morosini's own bombardment of the town from these heights had shown that this position was now the key to Nafplio's security. The long term solution could only be to fortify the entire mountain overlooking the town. Work on such a massive project finally began in 1711 and was substantially complete by 1714.

The rocky slopes of Palamidi precluded the construction of a conventional bastioned trace surrounded by a system of ditches.[2] The innovative solution chosen consisted of a network of semi-independent forts or bastions positioned to command all possible approaches to the heights above the town. Only two short ditches were constructed at either end of the Doppia Tenaglia. These were cut laboriously through the solid rock. The components of the complex are built in a

Summary

consistent architectural style similar to the land front of the town, with massive, rusticated blocks at the corners of each bastion.[3] The Bastione S. Girardo and the Bastione Staccato are essentially tall freestanding gun towers. Elsewhere the walls of the bastions form revetments to the natural slopes of the hill to heighten the exterior faces and ensure command of the ground beyond. Extensive use is made of brick in the embrasures of the main batteries. Throughout the complex the numerous loopholes for small arms, often built within a band of brick, are typically square internally but with two, three or four external apertures to give a variety of narrowly defined firing angles. Gates are placed at the rear of each work with posterns carefully concealed in their flanks.

The fall of Nafplio to Ottoman forces in 1715 began when the Turks exploded a mine against the southwest corner of the Doppia Tenaglia. Although this did little real damage it precipitated the flight of the garrison to the lower town. Nafplio's capitulation was caused by a failure of the garrison's nerve, exacerbated by a chronic shortage of manpower, rather than any defects in the fortifications. Nevertheless the Turks set about further improvements to the Palamidi complex. They completed the partially built eastern walls connecting the Piattaforma with the Doppia Tenaglia and the central main gate. In order to protect the ridge to the south of the Doppia Tenaglia that they themselves had occupied during their attack they constructed a new outwork, Fort Phokion, with yet more gun batteries at its southern tip. Built in a style similar to that of the Venetians, this was the last major work of fortification at Nafplio.

The appearance of the defences of the town and acropolis today owes much to the work of Wulf Schaefer. He was responsible for the restoration of the Bourtzi, although its conversion into a hotel was also to his design. The re-discovery of the east gate of the Castle of the Franks and its frescoes was entirely due to his personal efforts albeit at the cost of the destruction wrought by the building of the first access road. His drawings and ideas seem to have influenced much 20C restoration work. The reconstruction of the parapets of the Gambello traverse and its gate complex are based directly on his work and the recreation of the land gate utilised his architectural drawings. His surveys ensured that the appearance of the acropolis was recorded before the demolition of the Venetian military infrastructure and its replacement by modern hotels.

Summary

Notes

1. The circuit surrounding the lower town followed the model of thick battered walls interspersed with round towers with artillery platforms on the roof. By 1500 when the sea walls were completed, the defences when viewed from the harbour probably resembled those of Nafpaktos. Here the town walls were built around 1470 and have remained little changed and relatively intact to this day. Brooks, *Castles of Northwest Greece*, pp. 20-31.
2. The difficulty of digging in the rock of the hillside would have been an equal problem for any potential attacker.
3. In contrast the minor fort at Drepanon, completed at about the same time but standing in an isolated location, was built without embellishment.

Bibliography

Andrews, K., *Castles of the Morea*, The American School of Classical Studies at Athens (2006).
Βασιλείου, Α. and Μπουντούρης, Κ., *Ναυπλιο: Σημείωμα για την εξέλιξη της πόλης*, 25th Ephorate of Byzantine Antiquities (2010).
Bon, A., *The Medieval Fortifications of Acrocorinth and Vicinity, Corinth III, part II*, Cambridge, Mass. (1936).
Brooks, A., *Castles of Northwest Greece*, Huddersfield, Aetos (2013).
Brue, B., *Journal de la campagne que le Grand Vesir a faite en 1715 pour La Conquête de la Morée,* Paris (1872).
Caraher, R. C. and Gregory, T. E., *Fortifications of Mount Oneion, Corinthia*, Hesperia 75, No. 3 (2006).
DeVries, K. and Douglas, S. R., *Medieval Military Technology,* University of Toronto Press (2012).
Finlay, G., *The History of Greece under Othoman and Venetian Domination,* Edinburgh (1856).
Gerola, G., *Le Fortificazioni di Napoli di Romania*, Annuario della Regia Scuola di Archeologia di Atene, XIII-XIV (1930-31), pp. 347-410.
Gertwangen, R., *Fiscal and Technical Limitations on Venetian Military Engineering in the Stato Da Mar in the Fourteenth and Fifteenth Centuries,* in B. Lenman (ed.), Military Engineers and the Development of the Early-Modern European State, Dundee University Press (2013).
Hirschbichler, M., *The Crusader Paintings in the Frankish Gate At Nauplia, Greece: A Historical Construct in the Latin Principality of Morea*, Gesta XLIV/1 (2005), pp. 13-30.
Leake, W. M., *Travels in the Morea, Vol. II*, London (1830).
Lock, P., *The Franks in the Aegean 1204-1500,* London, Longman (1995).
Lurier, H. E., *Crusaders as Conquerors: the Chronicle of the Morea*, Columbia University Press (1964).
Mallett, M.E. and Hale, J.R., *The Military Organisation of a Renaissance State: Venice c.1400 to 1617*, Cambridge University Press (1984).
Mauro, M., *La Rocca di Ravenna,* Ravenna (1999).
McCleod, W. E., *Kiveri and Thermisi,* Hesperia 31, No. 4 (1962).
Miller, W., *Essays on the Latin Orient,* Cambridge (1921).
Miller, W., *The Latins in the Levant,* New York (1908).

Bibliography

Miller, W., *The Turkish Restoration in Greece, 1718-1797*, London (1921).
Mola, L., *Inventors, Patents and the Market for Innovations in Renaissance Italy*, History of Technology 32 (2014), pp. 7-34.
Μπάμπης, Αντωνιάδης «*Ημερολόγια» φυλακών της πόλης του Ναυπλίου*, Argolikis Archival Library History and Culture, https://argolikivivliothiki.gr/2011/11/06/ημερολόγια-φυλακών-της-πόλης-του-να/
Negris, P., *Vestiges Antiques Submergés*, Athens (1904).
Pepper, S., *Fortress and Fleet: The Defence of Venice's Mainland Greek Colonies in the Late Fifteenth Century*, in D.S. Chambers, C.H. Clough and M.E. Mallet (eds.), War, Culture and Society in Renaissance Venice, London (1993).
Sagredo, Agostino, *Report to the Venetian Senate*, Δελτίον Ιστορικής και Εθνολογικής Εταιρείας της Ελλάδος V, pp. 742-745.
Schaefer, W., *Das Stadttor von Akronauplia*, in W. Reusch (ed.), Neue Ausgrabungem im Nahen Osten, Mittelmeerraum und in Deutschland, Koldewey Gesellschaft (1959), pp. 18-24.
Schaefer, W., *Neue Untersuchungen über die Baugeschichte Nauplias im Mittelalter*, Jahrbuch des Deutschen Archäologischen Instituts und Archäologischer Anzeiger LXXVI (1961), pp. 156-214.
Schaefer, W., *Venezianische Festungsbaukunst in Griechenland. Zum Ausbau der Festung Nauplia*, Architectura 18 (1988), pp. 7-13.
Topping, P., *Venice's Last Imperial Venture*, Proceedings of the American Philosophical Society, Vol. 120 (1976).
Veikou, M., *Mediterranean Byzantine Ports and Harbours in the Complex Interplay between Environment and Society*, in J. Preiser-Kapeller and F. Daim (eds.), Harbours and Maritime Networks as Complex Adaptive Systems, Mainz (2015), pp. 39-60.
Wright, D. G., *Bartolomeo Minio: Venetian Administration in 15th Century Nauplion*, Electronic Journal of Oriental Studies III (2000), no. 5, www.let.uu.nl/oosters/EJOS/EJOS-III.5.html via the Wayback Machine.
Wright, D. G. and Melville-Jones, J.R., *The Greek Correspondence of Bartolomeo Minio Vol. 1 :Dispacci from Nauplion, 1479-1483*, Padua (2008)
Wright, D. G., *www.surprisedbytime.blogspot.com*
Zäh, A., *Venezianische Baugeschichte von Nauplia 1685-1715*, Südost-Forschungen Issue 68 (2009), pp. 138-183.
Zangger, E., *Landscape Changes around Tiryns during the Bronze Age*, American Journal of Archaeology 98 (1994), pp. 189-212.

Index

Acrocorinth, 3, 4, 6, 9 n.23, 63 n.3

Acronauplia 1, 5, 6, 7, 14, 20, 28, **41-65**; barracks, 6, 7, 47, 59, 60, 133; cavalry stables, 47, 59; Dolfin demi-bastion, 47, 49, 60; Gambello traverse & gate, 45, 46, 55-58, 65 n.24, 132, 134; Gambello postern, 58; military hospital, 7, 55; polygonal walls, 11, 41, 61; powder magazine, 59, 75; Sagredo gate, 11, 47, 60; use as a prison, 7; west gate, 20, 61; western gun battery, 61; WWII gun emplacements, 63; Xenia hotels, 7, 49

Argos, 1, 3, 4, 5, 7 n.7, 43, 123; plain of, 8. n.7, 8 n.16, 11, 13, 123, 126

Arvanitia, 18; gulley and bridge, 91

Athens, 4, 5, 7

Barbaro, Zaccaria, 46, 64 n.12

Bastione S. Girardo (see Fort Andreas)

Bastione Staccato (see Fort Miltiades)

Bayezid II, Sultan, 4

Bourtzi, xii, 4, 14, 25, **33-40**, 56, 132, 134; barbican, 34, 36, 39, 40 n.6, 56; central tower, 33, 39; north gate, 34, 36; porporella, 14, 16, 31 n.19; sea gate, 34, 36-37; used as an hotel, 33, 34, 39, 134

Brancaleone, 39 n.1

de Brienne, Walter, 3, 123

Castel del Toro, 4, 7, 11, 13, 14, 16, 17, 18, 28, 29, 30, 46, 47, 49, 51, 132, 133; Grimani battery, 47, 49, 51; Pasqualigo's gate, 46, 51-52; sally ports, 46, 47, 49, 51

Castello dello Scoglia (see Bourtzi)

Castle of Roumeli, 4, 5

Castle of the Franks, 3, 4, 7, 14, 41, 43, 45, 46, 47, 49, 51, 52, 53, 58, 132, 134; demi-lune, 52-53; east wall and gate, 41, 43, 45, 46, 47, 49, 53-54, 63 n.4, 134; Frankish tower, 41, 58, 63 n.3; frescoes, 43, 54, 63 n.4, 134; Venetian talus, 45, 46, 52, 53, 132; Venetian gate of 1471, 54-55

Castle of the Greeks, 3, 7, 14, 41, 43, 47

Index

Castle of the Morea, 4, 9 n.23
Castle of Roumeli, 4
Chania, 5
Chios, 6
Cittadella, Luigi, 18
Constantinople, xi, 3, 4
Corinth, 3, 5,4 6, 9 n.23; Isthmus, 4, 6, 9 n.22, 9 n.23; Gulf, 4, 6, 9 n.23
Cornaro, Pietro, 3
Cyprus, 5
Damokratidas of Argos, 1
Diedo, Vittorio, 22
Dolfin, Daniele, 18, 47
Doppia Tenaglia (see Fort Achilles)
Drepanon, xii, 22, **118-122**, 132, 135 n.3; cistern, 118, 119, 121
d' Enghien. Marie, 3, 123
Ermioni (see Kastri)
d' Este, Bertoldo, 4
Fort Achilles, 68, 86, 88, **91-97**, 112, 116, 133, 134; casemates, 91, 92, 97; gun platform, 91, 92, 95; postern gate, 97; rock cut ditch, 91, 95, 102; Turkish siege, 95, 114-115, 116 n.3
Fort Andreas, 66, 68, 69, 73, **75-82**, 85, 105, 108, 134; bell tower, 78; casemates, 81, 82; chapel, 81; cistern, 81; main gate, 76, 78; north demi-bastion, 75, 76, 78, 79, 81, 82; Piazza d'Armi, 75; postern gate, 75, 79; west demi-bastion, 79, 81, 82
Fort Epaminondas, 69, 76, 85, 91, 107, **112-116**; Turkish emblem, 115

Fort Leonidas, 69, 78, **107-111**, 112, 134; barrack block, 108-111, 117 n.14; cisterns, 111, 117 n.15; gates, 108; gun batteries, 107-108
Fort Miltiades, 66, 69, 88, **102-107**, 111, 115, 134; cistern, 105; outer courtyard, 103; postern gate, 103; sentry boxes, 107
Fort Phokion, 66, 68, 95, **97-101**, 134; cistern, 99; gun platforms, 99-101; casemates, 101; Venetian countermine, 97; postern gate, 101; Venetian ravelin, 68, 97
Fort Robert, **69-75**; postern gate, 72; powder magazine, 75; screen wall & stairway, 70, 72, 73, 75; stairway from lower town, 69-70
Fort Themistokles, 68, 69, 75, **82-91**, 95, 97, 102; barracks, 85; casemates, 86, 88; cistern, 85-86; gate, 85; gate to Doppia Tenaglia, 88; gun platform, 86, 88; rock-cut ditch, 86; postern gate, 88
Gambello, Antonio, 4, 14, 33, 39 n.1, 45
Gerola, Guiseppe, 12, 13, 22, 24, 33, 34, 40 n.6, 47, 64 n.12
Giaxich, 66, 68, 116 n.1
Glarentza, 13
Grimani, Francesco, 17, 20, 28, 31 n.25, 47, 66, 118
Hexamilion, 4
Holy League, 5
Kalamata, 4
Karathonas, 17

Index

Karlowitz, treaty of, 6, 9 n.22, 17
Kastri, 5, 123, 131 n.4
Kiveri, 3, 8 n.7, 8 n.16
Königsmark, Field Marshal, 5
Koroni, 3, 5
LaSalle, engineer, 18
Leake, William, 6
Lepanto, 4, 5, 131 n.10, 135 n.1; battle of, 5
Lerna, 8 n.7
Levasseur, Francoise, 18
Maschio (see Fort Robert)
Megara, 9 n.22
Mehmet II, Sultan, 4
Messenia, 3, 5
Methoni, 3, 4, 5, 17, 47; Bembo bastion, 47
Mezzo-baloardo S. Agostino (see Fort Themistokles)
Minio, Bartolomeo, 8 n.17, 16, 17, 46, 123, 131 n.6
Mocenigo, Alvise, 18
Monemvasia, 5
Morea (Peloponnese), xi, xii, 3, 4, 5, 6, 13, 31 n.25, 118, 123, 133
Morosini, Francesco, 5, 17, 20, 61, 66, 133
Murad II, Sultan, 3
Nafpaktos (see Lepanto)
Nafplio town; aqueduct, 17, 20, 31 n.21; battery of the Marina, 16, 18, 133; Byzantine, xi, 1, 3, 7 n.1, 12, 13, 14, 30 n.6, 41, 43, 54, 61, 63 n.2; capital of the Morea, 5, 6, 133; caponier, 20, 66, 69; cistern of the port, 20, 25; Contarina tower, 14, 16, 17, 18, 26, 133; district of the Marina, 26; Dolfin bastion, 7, 18, 26, 27; dredging of the harbour, 11, 20, 132; Five Brothers bastion, 14, 22, 24, 25; Franks, xi, 3, 8 n.7, 8 n.16, 13, 41, 43, 45, 57, 123, 132; Gate of the Marina, 16; Gate of the Ovens, 24; Gate of the Piazza, 25; Grimani bastion, 7, 18, 27-29, 30, 31 n.21, 49, 51, 66, 69, 133; Land walls & gate, xii. 4, 6, 7, 8 n.17, 13, 14, 16, 17, 18, 26-27, 29, 46, 68, 133, 134; Mocenigo bastion, 7, 18, 20, 26, 27, 133; Mycenaean, 1; Port, xi, 1, 6, 11-12, 13, 14, 16, 17, 20, 33, 41, 43, 132; Posto, 32 n.31; S. Nicolo, 16; S. Theresa bastion, 25; Strombolo tower, 14; territorial extent, 7 n.7, 8 n.16, 9 n.22 and 23; terraglio, 16; tower and gate of S. Maria of the Grotto, 22, 132; sea walls, 4, 6, 7, 8 n.17, 14, 16, 20, 26, 135 n.1; Turkish Nafplio, xi, 5, 6, 17, 24-25, 33
Navarino, 5, 131 n.10
Negris, Phocion, 12, 30 n.6
Negroponte, 3, 4, 5
Oneion, Mount, 9 n.23
Palamidi, xi. 1, 5, 6, 14, 17, 18, 20, 27, 31 n.21, 49, 66-117, 121, 133-134; use as a prison, 66, 103
Pasqualigo, Vettore, 4, 14, 16, 22, 33, 45, 46, 47, 51
Patras, 4
Pausanias, xi, 1
Petidis, Greek engineer, 55, 65

Index

n.25
Piattaforma, (see Fort Leonidas)
Preveza, battle of, 5
Pylos (see Navarino)
Ravenna, 39 n.1,
de la Roche, Otho, 3
Ruzzini, Carlo, 9 n.22
Sagredo, Agostino, 32 n.31, 47, 49, 66, 112, 116 n.2, 117 n.12, 118
Schaefer, Wulf, 11, 12, 33, 34, 41, 43, 49, 53, 55-56, 57, 63, n.3, 63 n.4, 65 n. 25, 134
Second World War, 33, 63
Sgouros, Leon, 3
Sgouros, Theodore, 3
Strabo, 1
Suleiman I, Sultan, 5, 16
Thermisi, 3, 4, 5, 8 n.7, 8 n.16, **123-131**, 133; Byzantine chapel, 127, 130 n.1; cistern, 126-127; inner bailey, 124, 126, 128, 129, 130; outer bailey, 124, 126, 128, 129-130; salt pans, xii, 126
Tiryns, 30 n.4
Tolon, 5, 17
Tripolitsa (Tripoli), 6, 9 n.26, 9 n.27
Turkish bastion, Palamidi (see Fort Phokion)
Turks, xi, 3-5, 6, 16, 17, 20, 24-25, 33, 43, 49, 56, 66, 68, 95, 97, 112, 114, 115, 116 n.3, 123, 130, 131 n.10, 133, 134
Venetian - Turkish wars, 4, 5-6, 16, 17, 43, 123; Ottoman reconquest 1715, 6, 66, 95, 97, 112, 114, 118, 123, 134
Venice, Venetians, xi, xii, 3, 4, 5, 6, 7, 7 n.1,8 n.7, 9 n.22, 9 n.23, 13, 14, 16, 17, 20, 22, 24, 25, 26, 27, 43, 47, 52, 54, 66, 68, 75, 97, 116 n.3, 118, 123, 126, 130, 132, 133; galleys, 16
De Villehardouin, Geoffrey I, 3
War of Independence, 7, 33, 66
Zen, Marco, 8 n.18

www.ingramcontent.com/pod-product-compliance
Lightning Source LLC
Chambersburg PA
CBHW031149160426
43193CB00008B/301